What people are
SoulW<

What makes *SoulWorks* such a useful book is that it deals in terms of themes that run through people's lives rather than simply the narratives. Lives do have patterns, there is a direction – and when we tune into these deeper structures, we get a sense of meaning which can then inform everything we do. The result is often a profound shift rather than a superficial change.

Jane also has the gift for expressing complex truths simply, for making the abstruse accessible. This is a must read for anyone interested in self-development, the mind and the way we function as human beings in the world.
Dr Shomit Mitter, M.Phil (Oxon), PhD (Cantab), www. shomitmitter.com

SoulWorks is about rediscovering your personal potential to the absolute best of your ability. It combines Western and Eastern approaches to psychology and philosophy which inspire you to create your very own life story. There are plenty of practical exercises to help readers apply their new-found wisdom to everyday situations. Jane writes with empathy and insight, and this book makes an original contribution to the popular field of spiritual development.

If you're at a crossroads in your life looking for a new approach, *SoulWorks* provides both inspiration and practical guidance.
Anna Cherry, The Habitat Affect

If you've fallen foul of the Western dilemma of disillusionment with what you have, then this is surely the antidote. Practical, pragmatic and concise, this book is backed by science, anecdote

and experience. Jane's work cleverly weaves together nuggets of wisdom from sources as wide-ranging as Carl Jung, Joseph Campbell and Buddhism. Discover what matters to you; what's truly important; what brings you joy and nourishment. Live passionately. Live purposefully. Live your Soul Story.
Bridget Finklaire, Consultant Therapist

Using tried and tested exercises and her in-depth understanding of myth and traditional tales, Jane Bailey Bain offers you a simple yet profound way to explore your own soul story.
John Kent, Director, Voice Dialogue UK

This is a beautiful book which can really help people. It has a wealth of interesting connections about the mind, body, soul and makes fascinating links with music and myth, interwoven with the author's personal reflection. The book provides practical steps and visualisations to engage the reader in doing the work, moving them forward to having more agency in their life experience.
Miranda Kersley, Clinical Psychotherapist, Counsellor & Life Coach

The theme of the 'soul story' in which associations between people, places and events bring deep and multifaceted meaning to our lives is very important to good mental health. Often people in crisis are poor historians of their own lives. Recovery comes when they are able to explore their past, the influences and experiences that have shaped them: in other words, to first discover and then narrate their own stories. Jane provides inspiration for us all, as well as practical resources to guide us through the hurly-burly of everyday life.
Gillian Wood, MBPsS

A fresh and accessible perspective upon an important topic for an age of seismic changes. Right now, identity and purpose are centrally important to personal evolution and success in self-discovery and development. Jane provides a fresh approach for seekers of meaning.

Peter Urey, Director, Find Your Path In Life

Other Books by Jane Bailey Bain

LifeWorks

Why did your life turn out this way? Who are the most important people in your world? What would you do differently, if you had the chance? Ever since you were a child, you have been composing your own life script. You use fragments of story from books, films and magazines to weave your personal narrative. The characters in your script are acted by people around you, and you can choose who has a significant role. *LifeWorks* is a practical handbook which combines insights from psychology and anthropology. It shows you how to identify relationship patterns and life themes. You are the author of your story, and play the principal part. Once you are aware of this, you can start to direct your own life script.

978-1-78099-038-5 (Paperback)
978-1-78099-039-2 (e-book)

StoryWorks

StoryWorks is a practical handbook on how to tell stories. It ranges from classic tools like the 'Rule of Threes' to the new mnemonic 'Five Finger Technique'. There are creative exercises, applied resources, and many stories to expand your narrative repertoire. When you have something to say, the best way to communicate is by telling a story. This book shows you how to do that effectively. Great writers know the power of narrative. Teachers and trainers use words as a tool for transformation. If you're a writer wanting to improve your skills, a coach or leader looking for new ideas, a teacher working with young people – this book will help you tell better stories.

978-1-78279-986-3 (Paperback)
978-1-78279-987-0 (e-book)

SoulWorks

Living Your Soul Story

SoulWorks

Living Your Soul Story

Jane Bailey Bain

BOOKS

Winchester, UK
Washington, USA

First published by O-Books, 2018
O-Books is an imprint of John Hunt Publishing Ltd., No. 3 East St., Alresford,
Hampshire SO24 9EE, UK
office1@jhpbooks.net
www.johnhuntpublishing.com

For distributor details and how to order please visit the 'Ordering' section on our website.

Text copyright: Jane Bailey Bain 2017

ISBN: 978 1 78535 713 8
978 1 78535 714 5 (ebook)
Library of Congress Control Number: 2017936417

A CIP catalogue record for this book is available from the British Library.

Design: Stuart Davies

Printed and bound by CPI Group (UK) Ltd, Croydon, CR0 4YY, UK

We operate a distinctive and ethical publishing philosophy in
all areas of our business, from our global network of authors to
production and worldwide distribution.

Contents

For Kyrian, Wulfie and Annapurna

Preface

Your life has a thread. It tells where you've been and what you've done. It shows how one incident led to another. It explains how things turned out this way.

But your life has a deeper story. This one links the people, places and events that matter to you. It shows how your encounters follow patterns. It relates your actions to your inner values.

This story emphasizes themes and motifs. It lets you see connections between things. It shows how early experiences link to later ones. It helps you understand what really matters.

Once you see this, you'll start to live quite differently. You'll spend more time on things that are important. You'll become aware of themes and patterns in your life. You'll want to focus on learning and giving, experiences and relationships.

This deeper narrative is your soul story.

Part I

Only those who will risk going too far can possibly find out how far one can go.
– TS Elliot

Soul Story

Who are you? It's a hard question to answer. If I turn it back on myself, I don't have a simple reply. I'm not my name, though that's how I introduce myself. I'm not just my body, though that's what you see when you look at me. So what is the right answer to this question?

It might help to break it down into smaller parts. Who are you? – could mean:

What is your name?
Where do you live?
What do you do for a living?
Why do you get up in the morning?
What sports do you enjoy?
What music makes you dance?
Who do you spend time with?
What really matters to you?
How do you feed your soul?
What is your life purpose?

All these things are part of you. None of them defines you but they all express something about you. When you make a new friend, you learn these things about them. Sometimes you learn from doing things together. Other things you learn through talking – conversations where you share what's important to you. Little bits of information fall into place like a mosaic. Gradually you build up a picture of who they are.

How exactly does this happen? When you meet someone new, the first impression is physical: how they look, how they dress, how they carry themselves. When you're a child, these things seem largely pre-ordained: you're born with straight or curly hair and a certain amount of confidence. As you grow up, you learn to manipulate that image. You can dye your hair, go to the gym, practise smiles for selfies. You play with the picture that people get when they first meet you.

The first thing that people see is your appearance. Knowing this, you can decide what image to project. You choose what clothes to wear, what accessories to carry, whether to smile or stay aloof. You judge other people by their appearance too, because that's their message to the world. Even when you meet someone online, you want to see their picture. It's a normal human instinct to rely on vision: about eighty per cent of your information about the world comes through your eyes. So the physical body that you inhabit is an important part of how you relate to the world.

The second aspect of identity is what you think. This is how you relate to the world on an intellectual level. As you get to know someone, your relationship moves beyond appearances. You start to become interested in them as a person. You want to find out more about them – things that can't be seen with the eyes alone. Physical presence is no longer enough. For the bond to deepen, you have to connect on another level. This stage is where you get to know a person properly. You learn more about each other and forge a lasting relationship. The way you do this still uses a physical medium – talking – but it's a connection involving your minds.

The third pillar of existence is spiritual. This is the part of you which balances mind and body. Your soul exists in the plane of cosmic energy. When you relate with another soul, they touch the core of your being. Soul connection occurs without your conscious choice. Sometimes it goes against logic, practicality, common sense. For soul connections are uncommon. If you're lucky, you'll have a handful in your whole life. If you're very lucky indeed, you'll find a soul mate – your true partner. When you forge soul connections, you have people who will always matter, even when you are apart. These are friends who reflect the depths of your being. They hold you safely in their hearts, as you do them. They are a fundamental part of your soul story.

What is your soul story? On one level, it's the story of your life. It has a physical basis: it takes place in time and space. It records what happened to you, and when, and where. If you tell this story to other people, it relates where you've been and what you've done. Of course, your narrative is selective. You'll highlight some things – the ones that seem significant – and erase others. But overall, it's a factual autobiography.

On another level, your story is a way of explaining your experiences. You analyse what happened on an intellectual level: why things turned out for you as they did. When you go over this story in your mind, it explains why you are the way you are. It's a way of understanding your behaviour and emotional responses. This is the basis for much therapy, and it can bring some interesting insights.

Your soul story is based on life events and logical analysis, but it's much more than this. It's what underlies the first and last questions above – Who are you? and, What is the purpose of your existence? Your soul story is the unique fabric of your life. It connects the people, places and events that matter in your narrative. It has patterns that bridge external events and transcend intellectual analysis. It weaves your being on all three levels: physical, mental and spiritual. It's a narrative that brings together the key themes of your existence.

When you tell your soul story, you know yourself at last. You have a deep sense of fulfilment and meaning in life. Your mind is opened to a higher reality. You see links that connect things outside direct causation. You start trusting your intuition. You experience feelings of love, joy and abundance. You know what matters and what you're meant to do. You find a conviction that gives you strength. No matter what your beliefs, you glimpse a cosmic truth outside human comprehension. When you tell this story, it's like coming home.

Your soul story can be told in words, but it won't follow a single narrative thread. Soul stories operate outside simple verbal sequences. That's because the patterns manifest in multiple dimensions. Each time you contemplate your story, you'll see something new. Overlay the story with repeated re-tellings and you'll see how it works at many levels. When you learn the stories of significant others, your soul companions, you'll find they resonate with yours. They touch and interweave, occupying the same time and space on different levels. Your connection with them isn't a matter of choice but of recognition. It's no surprise that these people are significant in your life.

Soul stories don't obey the rules of time and space. Those are aspects of the mind and body. They are useful constructs for daily life, but they do not define your story. In your soul story, the end defines the beginning rather than the start determining the end. The different elements of your story exist simultaneously. To understand this, picture a piece of fabric. The pattern was planned from the beginning, but it only appeared after it was woven. You can pick up the edges of the fabric and touch them together. A beetle crawling across the cloth would experience the two ends as being next to each other. It's the same with your soul's experience of your life.

You can see how this works from fairy tales. These are stories which have stood the test of time. They have survived because they resonate with us on a deep level. In fairy tales, the narrative elements are utterly familiar: that is to say, they exist in our minds simultaneously. This is precisely what gives them resonant power. We know from the start that Little Red Riding Hood will defy the wolf, that Sleeping Beauty will awake, that Jack will kill the giant. These things don't invalidate the story; rather, they add depth and meaning to each narrative element.

Another way of envisaging your soul story is as a ballad. Like music, it has an opening and a closing; a melody, rhythm and counterpoint. The melody is a sequence of notes like the storyline. The rhythm gives momentum to the tune. Musical phrases are echoed, giving depth and pattern. And as for the repeated chorus... have you ever felt that you kept getting the same lessons in life? These are the key themes that you need to work on, to become the person that you're meant to be. So another way of expressing your life purpose is 'singing your soul song'.

Like music, your soul story is meant to be experienced in the moment. You don't live a story for its ending, any more than you listen to a symphony for the final chord. Alan Watts says, 'We thought of life as a journey, and kept trying to reach a destination. But we missed the whole point: it was a musical thing, and you were supposed to sing or dance whilst the music was being played.' That's a good reminder to live in the present: to make the most of each moment in this life.

So who are you? You're a spiritual being inhabiting a physical body with a mental engine. The purpose of your existence is to create and express your soul story. And that is what you will learn to do here. You'll discover the five-fold structure of weaving your story:

- identifying who you want to be
- knowing where you're going
- plotting the stages of adventure
- key people: building relationships
- giving your gift to the world

You'll see how to weave these things together into a narrative that crosses space and time. This work will help you understand the past and create your chosen future. Your soul story brings together people, places, life events. It makes sense of your time here on earth. It gives your life joy, purpose and a deep sense of meaning.

You'll learn to sing the song you were born to sing.

The Parallel World

Look around you. All you see is a part of the manifest world. It operates with physical laws and scientific principles. Everything is clear, light, rational. In the everyday world you operate on a conscious level. Cause and response are plain to see. If you act in a certain way, you know what will happen.

There is another world which exists parallel to this one. It operates on spiritual principles and magical thinking. In this other world, you must respect wilder powers. Logical decisions have no weight; wisdom is valued, and heart's calling. This is the realm of the soul.

This parallel world has always been known to mystics and thinkers. The Celts spoke of an Otherworld which is contiguous with this one. At certain times of year, the veil between these worlds is thin: Beltane, which we call May Day; and Samhain, which we celebrate as Hallowe'en. At these times, visitors can cross easily from one realm to another. Mortal musicians might be asked to play for the faerie king; travellers could be given sustenance. If you are invited, the otherworld is a place of untold riches; but if you venture unannounced it is dangerous.

Most of the time, you live in the everyday world. It's easy to understand and clear to navigate. This is the world of the conscious mind. You know the rules and the penalties for breaking them. If you drop a glass, it breaks. If you steal a cake, you're punished. Social pressure forces you to toe the line. This world is generally referred to as 'reality'.

The other dimension has many names. Sometimes it's called the inner world, as though it has no connection to physical reality. It may be called the spirit realm, where other forces operate. Often it's dismissed as dream, or fantasy, or imagination. But this world matters more than anything outside yourself. It's where you compose your soul's story.

Everything that happens in your outer life is determined by this script. When you're living in line with your soul purpose, things go well. When you deny your soul's truth, you fail to flourish. For your life is given meaning through your soul story. You ignore this parallel world at your peril.

The language of the soul must be listened to carefully. The external world conditions you to look for causes. The soul operates more stealthily, through subtle correlations. Yet everyone receives messages from the spiritual realm. At times of change, challenge or crisis they come more strongly. If you respond to the call, you learn to hear it clearly.

What sort of event initiates the call? Some people hear it at puberty: they have to get up, leave the known, discover another world where they belong. Others experience it when someone close dies: their soul needs to spend time in the dark realm, grieving the loss. Sometimes it happens when you fall in love: the world is changed utterly, and you can never return to the state you were in before.

Heeding the call is dangerous. Once you're aware of your soul story, you cannot delete that consciousness. If you don't act on it, you'll have a quotidian life of minor disappointments. Gradually you'll lose your sense of self, caught in a state of spiritual paralysis. If you do respond, you're in for a roller-coaster ride. But follow the road less travelled, and finally it will lead you back to paradise.

That means to experience eternity in the present moment. Yeats said, 'There is another world, but it is in this one.' When you recognize this truth, you have found enlightenment. What happens before or after is not relevant. Living according to your soul story is to have heaven on earth.

If it's so simple, why doesn't everyone do it? Well, I warned you that it was a hard process. Many people never hear the call to spiritual awakening. If they do, they choose to ignore it: too much would be lost, too many people would get hurt. That's a very sensible attitude and I'd recommend it. After all, the spirit world is dangerous. Your soul is a wild thing: why else would you have come on this great adventure called life?

The signs of spiritual awakening are close to mania, or falling in love. You feel surges of energy through your body. You need far less sleep, often waking in the night. Your heart races for no apparent reason. Your tastes change: you're drawn towards natural foods, and might lose weight. Your skin glows and you seem to be growing younger. You have a heightened sensory appreciation: colours seem brighter, music more beautiful. You may take up singing or dancing, writing or drawing.

There are subtler changes too. In one way, you withdraw: you have no time for mindless socializing. At the same time you're more outgoing, connecting authentically with everyone you meet. You have a sense of one-ness and connectedness with humanity. With this comes increased integrity: you can't stay in a job or relationship that isn't true to your soul story. You start to unclutter – people, things, commitments – from your life.

And once you heed the inner call, the outer world conspires to help you. Strangers offer insights; training opportunities appear; you get a chance to make some money. Even apparent setbacks have a purpose. You miss the train and meet a friend on the next one. You lose a job and find you're free to travel. Teachers appear with perfect timing: messages manifest everywhere – in books, films, even on the news.

When you're living your soul story, the two worlds synchronize. Mind and soul work together to create a new reality. The universe cooperates with your personal transformation. Psychologist Carl Jung writes about a woman who dreamed of a scarab, symbol of regeneration, and found one tapping at the window. He believed that such meaningful coincidence was a key part of personal growth.

So you move forward in the direction of your dreams. This is all very disconcerting for the people around you. You seem different, and that threatens their own life choices. They don't want you to change, because they could lose you. They have a vested interest in keeping you exactly how you are. Expect huge social pressure not to alter anything. Really you shouldn't make any rash decisions. Surely you can go on living as it was?

But you can't, and you shouldn't even consider it. If you try to compromise, the old ways will close around you like a trap. You must be true to your soul's calling: you must follow the pattern of your soul story. That's what the work here is all about.

For the things we regret most in life are the choices not made, the chances not dared, the risks not taken. However things turn out, you'll learn from the experience. If you act, you'll find the confidence to live your dreams.

Look around, take stock and consider your options. Put in place what's necessary to safeguard those you care for. Put on your wingsuit and adjust the fastenings. Take a deep breath. Let go.

You'll never find out if you can fly until you jump.

We have not even to risk the adventure alone: for the heroes of all time have gone before us. The labyrinth is thoroughly known... We have only to follow the thread of the hero path. And where we had thought to find an abomination, we shall find a god. And where we had thought to slay another, we shall slay ourselves. Where we had thought to travel outwards, we shall come to the centre of our own existence. And where we had thought to be alone, we shall be with all the world.

– Joseph Campbell, *The Hero's Journey*

The Science of SoulWork

Your soul story is the theme of your life. It explains who you are, dictates what you should do and shows where you should go. So it's important that you believe it matters. Before we start work on your story, let's take a quick look at the science that underlies it.

Body, mind and soul: these are the three pillars of your existence. Your body performs in the physical world. Your mind functions on the mental plane. Your soul comes from the spiritual realm. Together, they form the 'self' as which you operate in this manifest world.

Your body, mind and soul are intimately connected. You have a physical body which interacts with the outer world. You have a mental operating system which lets you control your body and affect external reality. And you have a soul, which connects with the physical world through your mind and body, but transcends both.

Your body and mind change over time, as a result of both external forces and conscious manipulation. Your physical self is a concrete manifestation of energy. It is a transient phenomenon. You can shape it with diet and training, but it is designed for a limited journey. In technical terms, the body has built-in obsolescence. Ultimately outer forces will prevail and your body in its current form will cease to exist.

Your mind is like an operating system for the body. It allows you to channel energy through thought and implementation to affect the material world. In order to operate efficiently, the mind creates a self-contained explanatory system. You experience this creation as 'me': some people identify this as their ultimate reality. However, your mind is impermanent, created for a specific incarnation. Already it slips in and out of consciousness when you sleep. When the neural wiring disappears, your mind as you know it will cease to exist.

Your soul is an aspect of cosmic energy. It existed before you were born; it will ultimately leave your body. It comes from a realm without speech, so it is difficult to describe verbally. You sense it in the spaces – the pause between words, the gap between actions, the empty chair and the open road. Sanskrit texts call it Atman, the seat of the self. It is the purposer of life, your alpha and omega, the reason you became incarnate. Your soul song is the template for your time here on earth.

How can we see these three levels working? Let's look at this empirically. You're fairly convinced that your body exists. On a functional level, this is easily evident: scratch yourself, and it hurts. Your mind also seems fairly incontrovertible. Sometimes the inside of your head seems more real than the external world. The soul's existence is more difficult to prove. By definition it's subjective, because it is your 'self'. It reveals itself in subtle ways: dreams and visions, premonitions and intuitions. All of these are manifestations of cosmic energy. And energy by definition manifests through movement: positive and negative, joining and separating, forwards and backwards. All of these are aspects of relationship. So a good way of studying interpersonal energies is through your relationships with others.

Physical, mental and spiritual: these are the dimensions of a good relationship. When you connect with your bodies, you have physical attraction. When you connect with your minds, you have intellectual compatibility. When you connect with your souls, you have true friendship. When you have all three, you have the potential for lasting love. But are these connections 'real'? Maybe you think love is an illusion: something we imagine because no-one wants to be alone. Let's look at the science and see how it works.

When you touch someone physically, it forms a connection between you. The touch might be anything from a casual brush to a full-body hug. The feeling can range from a small fuzz to a lightning strike. It's a very real sensation, and it has a tangible effect on the body. That's because we're all made of atoms. Any level of contact causes a flow of energy. When you sense these electric impulses, they operate like nerve impulses generated inside the body. Your brain arranges the release of neurotransmitters – oxytocin, cortisol, dopamine – which cause a physical response. You experience this response as emotion, arousal, excitement. Touching someone literally lets your bodies interconnect.

When two minds meet, something similar happens. You don't need physical contact to conduct electricity. The most dramatic example of this is lightning. In fact, even nerves inside the body don't actually connect: the electrical impulse jumps over a tiny gap at each junction. (There's a good reason for this design: if neural pathways were all set at birth, it would be much harder to repair or develop new networks.) When you are on the same 'wavelength' as someone, you can share thoughts without putting them into words. Is this a crazy new age idea? Not according to neurological research. Experiments at Washington and Harvard using transcranial magnetic stimulation (TMS) show that telepathy is a real phenomenon.

So far, so good: but what about the spirit? When you have that soul connection, it is truly magical. That is to say, it transcends the laws of our phenomenal world – as do the findings of modern science.

Quantum physics shows that we are all part of a universal energy field. Some of this energy manifests as matter; some as heat; and some as light. Energy is never created or destroyed; it merely changes form. This is how plants make food out of sunlight. Photosynthesis is the basis for life on earth. But it doesn't transform energy, merely its appearance. You were probably taught at school that everything is made of atoms. At CERN, physicists study the basic units of matter. They have found that an atom is not a solid structure but a vortex of electric particles. So the great mystics were right: everything is made of energy.

It gets even better. Because electrical charges interact, each particle in the universe connects to every other particle. Once a quantum particle interacts with another particle, their states remain linked, even when they are far apart. This state is given the nice name of 'entanglement' (physicists are rather romantic like that). Quantum particles have various properties, including polarity and spin. A pair of quantum particles always have the opposite property to each other. When researchers change the polarity or spin of one particle, its twin changes too, no matter where they are.

This confirms Heisenberg's Uncertainty Principle: that the nature of matter is fundamentally unknowable. Things only exist in relation to each other. Underlying material form is nothing but energy. What really exists is not solid particles, but space. Matter is nothing but a connection between two entities. What matters is the relationship between things. This manifests in the observer effect: the moment you look at a subatomic particle, you influence its state. If you measure the speed of a particle, you can't be sure of its location – and vice versa.

This gives rise to one of my favourite jokes (I like it because it makes me feel clever). Heisenberg is speeding down the autobahn when a traffic cop pulls him over. The policeman says, "Sir, do you know how fast you were going?" Heisenberg replies, "No, but I know exactly where I was." The policeman is not impressed. "You were going at one hundred kilometres per hour!" Heisenberg looks crushed. "Shoosh," he says, "Now we're completely lost!"

Let's be clear: the universe is a unified energy field. Some of this energy lies outside the range of human perception. Animals can use infrared night vision which falls beyond our visible spectrum. But it can be detected by simple scientific equipment. Matter only exists as a web of energetic relationships. So everything in the world is made of electricity. This means that mental energy – the firing of neurons in your brain – is the same force that constitutes matter. If thought is a form of energy, it's not surprising that it can affect the phenomenal world.

From here it's only a small step to recognizing other forms of energy. The clearest and most widespread example is probably dowsing. It's well known that you can sense the presence of water using a forked stick. A friend who lives in the Orkneys mentioned recently how they had used a dowser to detect subterranean streams running under their land. In her community calling on the dowser is a commonplace affair. You can use a similar technique for detecting metal objects. I've felt the force myself and the pull is unmistakeable.

Physical, mental, spiritual: energy connects things on every level. And like every gift in a fairy tale, there's a downside if the power is misused. If our minds can communicate directly, they can also broadcast energy. If you don't control these emissions, you're not thinking about where they might end up. Like a child with a hosepipe, you're randomly spraying the world. Most of the time you're not even aware that you're doing it. Sending out signals you're not aware of is downright dangerous.

Once you understand this, you can start to control the process. The law of attraction is really a law of radiation. Transmitting energy in any form affects your surroundings. It follows that your thoughts impact the world around you. This is a great gift, but also a tremendous responsibility. There's no time out, no escape, no excuses. What you think about will come into your life.

Some people call this the 'law of attraction' and try to create wealth, or health, or a loving relationship. It's not quite so simple as that. Manifestation operates on a causal link, not a direct correlation. In this respect it's rather like karma: you can't order the result. If you think of something good (or bad), it won't immediately show up in your world. Nevertheless, whatever you focus on will materialize, even if you don't recognize it immediately. It may not be quite what you imagined, but it will appear in response to your thoughts.

You might be sceptical about this. The theory sounds nice, but it's not borne out by your experience. You've wished hard for something, but there hasn't been a sign of it. That could be because you're not directing your thoughts properly. Remember that you get what you focus on. Have you been thinking about the spaces in your life? Switch your mind to what you really want. As your attitude changes, so more things will be attracted to you. And the more you think about something, the more specific that manifestation will be.

What you're really learning here is a law of connection. On a physical level, the effects are obvious. If you pinch yourself, you experience physical pain; if you pinch someone else, they'll let you know about it. On the mental plane, a meeting of minds is a transformative experience. Debate, discussion, argument – exchanging ideas can lead you to change your thoughts. In the spiritual dimension, the communication is more subtle. Think back to times when you had a premonition, or an experience of déjà vu. Perhaps you've learned to follow your instincts: should you believe this person? If you've had experiences like these, you'll know you can trust your intuition. Train yourself to 'listen to the whispers'. Follow the small signs and you'll find a way even where no path was visible. With every step you'll feel the ground more firmly underfoot. Body, mind and spirit are all present and connected. Everything that manifests in your life is part of your soul story.

That's the science of soulwork. Now, let's start putting the theory into practice.

Doing the Practice

Ever since you were young, you've been working on your soul story. When you were a child, this was an unconscious process. You grew up somewhere, went to a certain school, did certain activities mainly as a result of someone else's decisions. The start of your story was determined by factors set in place before you were born. It doesn't matter whether you believe that you 'chose' these things: they are just part of your existential identity.

As you grew up, things started to throw you off track. Maybe there were family events that upset you: moving, divorce, losing someone. You set your sights on a certain goal and didn't get it; or you did, and it turned out not to be what you expected. Perhaps you followed other people's paths. Probably you compromised to do what was expected.

These comments all come from my own experience. Myself, I'm a perfectionist and try too hard. It comes across as headstrong and unheeding. I was torn between making everything right and following my own heart. When things sensed wrong, I used to flutter like a trapped bird. These days, I've learned to acknowledge what is instead of what should be. Then I step back from the closed door and look for an open window.

At this point in time, you may feel that you've lost direction. You tried following the standard path, and it petered out in the sand. Or you tried to make your own way until the undergrowth became impenetrable. Probably you've tried a mixture of the two. You need practical skills to find your way again. That's why this book contains more than just theory. There are activities to help you back onto the path, and to keep you heading in the right direction.

These exercises call on your inner resources. Some of them draw on the power of visioning; some call on your creative abilities; others on practical planning. They enlist your mind,

19

soul and body in a lifeline project. It's no good just reading about your soul story: you have to activate these processes.

Visioning works by drawing on the power of the subconscious mind. You'll start by getting into a state of deep relaxation. This lets your brain enter a condition of theta wave activity. In this state you can access both perception and intuition. You'll invite images and symbols which resonate with subliminal knowledge. These provide the strongest base for identifying your soul story.

Activities involving pencil and paper work with the conscious mind. Word games draw on the left side of the brain – your logical, sequential processing side. Drawing evokes the right side of the brain, associated with visual-spatial awareness. These two halves are connected by a bundle of nerves called the corpus callosum. When you combine these processes, your mind makes lightning linkages that surpass ordinary perception.

Exercises that involve the body aim to link you with external reality. As you've learned, there is a direct connection between the body and mind. Sensory perceptions affect your internal world; conversely, the mind can translate thoughts into activities. Consciously linking your physical and mental states allows you to directly manifest your soul story.

Play with the material and adapt it to your own needs. These activities can be done in any time or place. All of them can be done repeatedly, in any order. Approach them in a spirit of creativity and adventure. You'll gain different perspectives and insights each time you do them.

So Who Are You?

Or, living the life you want... and being the person you want to be.

So you know that you're responsible for creating your life. You're willing to work for the results you want. Now you're ready to start work on your soul story.

To live the life you want, you must be the sort of person who would live that life. It's no good dreaming you'll run with the wolves if you spend most nights watching television. That means your fantasy is just a passive dream. So let's turn the question backwards, and look at the person you want to be. Naturally that starts with who you are now. It's back to the Delphic admonition.

Who do you think you are? It's the most important question in your life. Your self image determines how you interact with the world. Are you cautious or daring? Independent or community oriented? Generous or more concerned with looking out for yourself? How you see yourself affects everything you do and every choice you make.

Your self image affects your behaviour in subtle ways. It influences how you interact with everyone you meet. Do you smile at strangers or avoid eye contact? Give money to buskers or hurry on home? You probably change from day to day but you'll have a constant style that reflects your character. It's what your friends would describe as your personality. It determines how you relate to the people around you. And those interactions, ranging from chance encounters to deep friendships, are what define your life.

This is really important because who you are determines what happens to you. Why is it that some people make friends everywhere they go? They always seem to have a wonderful time: their work is fascinating, they meet interesting people, their weekends are filled with picnics and parties. Your life seems drab by comparison. Actually, the difference is probably one of attitude. These people have the Midas touch: everything they encounter turns to gold. You want to be near them, so some of that fairy dust rubs off on you.

We're not talking about online media here, because most people know that's a social construct. For the gift to be real, it has to be a genuine attitude. If you ask someone like this how they always have such a good time, they might answer, "I decided to". Because appreciating life is most often a decision that was consciously made. It's not an act, but rather a deep commitment to living life to the full. Social contacts may get you invitations to glitzy parties, but wearing a ball gown is no guarantee of a good time. Really having fun – in a palace or a shanty town – is mainly up to you.

Your attitude affects how you interact with the people you meet. And meeting people is what brings choices into your life. This is a life lesson that really applies to me. I could write all day, but every few hours I go for a walk. When I get out, I meet people – saying hello to the cashier as I buy milk, running into a friend on the street, exchanging a few words with the guy next to me on the train. Each small encounter has the potential to teach you something new. They add up to a series of opportunities: chances which increase the choices that are available to you. And those choices link together to make a story.

If your choices make a story, then you can decide what happens next. Like it or not, you're mainly in charge of your life. Sure, from time to time fate sends a curved ball: you lose your job, the roof is leaking, your elderly parent gets sick. These things don't seem fair and you certainly didn't want them to happen. How can they possibly be under your control? But even if you're not responsible, you can still determine what happens next in your story. How? – it's very simple: how you respond to them is up to you.

Say the company you work for has decided to relocate

overseas. Is this a terrible blow or a wonderful adventure? If you don't want to move with them, perhaps that reflects how you feel about the job. Maybe this is a wonderful opportunity to rethink your career. If there's a redundancy deal, this could be your chance to set up as self-employed. Look at all your options and see how this could actually help develop your story. Instead of feeling like a victim, you can decide that this is the best thing that could have happened.

Of course, sometimes we jinx our own stories. We line everything up perfectly and then at the last minute we throw in the towel. I've done this quite a few times myself, so I know the dangers here. Well, hard luck – then you have to live with the consequences of your choices. And that's when your reactions really matter. Maybe life isn't how you envisaged it: the problem isn't with the world, it's the mismatch between your expectations and reality. You need to stop thinking about what you wish were true and focus on what really is.

And here we have an interesting dichotomy. It's vital to live in the moment: to appreciate the world as it really is. This is one of the oldest insights – ancient Sanskrit and Buddhist teachings emphasize this truism – and one of the newest, in the name of 'mindfulness'. It's why you feel better when you've been for a walk: being in nature helps us to feel 'presence' – living in the moment, not lost in labyrinths of the mind. It's summed up in the saying: 'The past is gone, the future is a dream, but now is a gift – that's why it's called the present.'

Yet at the same time it's important to hold on to your dreams. To think about them, focus on them, clarify the details and start working towards them. If you just leave them as fantasy, they will almost certainly never happen. If you take even the smallest steps, you will start to move in the right direction. As I'm writing this, my phone pings – it's a response from a new friend offering accommodation for a trip I want to make. If I hadn't made that first contact, it wouldn't be about to come true.

What's stopping you from taking that first step? Sometimes the dream doesn't seem worth fighting for: it would involve so much disruption, you're hardly sure it's worth the cost. Maybe there are other people to think about: a partner, or children, or colleagues who depend on you. Perhaps you're tied down by a mortgage or long-term debt. Possibly you're worried about your health, or whether you could cope with the uncertainty of starting out again.

In that case, you've got to sit down and think very clearly about what you want. It's no good keeping your daydream as a vague fallback option. That will only lead to discontent without actually prompting you to change anything. It's also quite possibly dangerous, because you'll get frustrated about how things aren't perfect. If you want your dream badly enough, go for it. If life is just complicated, decide whether you're going to act or if you'd actually prefer to live with it.

Other times, your dream is so huge, it seems crazy even to imagine it. What makes you think that you could ever deserve such fame/love/happiness? Follow that dream and you'll probably just end up looking stupid. In any case, you're not sure where to start. It seems impossible that you could ever achieve something so big. Even if it would be wonderful... especially if it would be wonderful. If you aim for the moon, you're likely to crash-land on your nose.

This fear of social embarrassment is a rather English attitude. Hollywood, in contrast, is full of people working as waiters who plan to direct movies. Actually you're just as likely as anyone else to achieve your dream, so long as you're willing to work for it. As Oscar Wilde famously commented, "I'm a great believer in luck; the harder I work, the more I seem to have." The trick here isn't to panic, it's actually to aim a little higher. No-one buys a lottery ticket hoping to get their money back. If you've dared to dream so far, go for the ultimate prize. When you aim for the stars, you've got a good chance of landing on the moon.

Say you believe in your dream, you're certain it's right for you, you've even thought about how to start putting it into action. Still it seems too daunting, too huge to ever actually achieve. You just don't feel up to it today – now hold that thought! No-one expects you to achieve everything all in one go. The important thing is to begin: to make a move in the right direction. As the Chinese say, every voyage starts with a single step.

So what do you want to do next? You can't live the same year ninety times and call it a life. And as we've seen, there's a dichotomy here: you can't live the life you want unless you're the person you want to be. So the only place to start is here and now. Everything begins with you as you are today, working towards who you want to be. Which is incredibly lucky, really: because you can't control outside events, you can't make other people behave how you want, but you can work out who you are... and decide who you're going to be.

Part II

Some people live their whole lives on the default settings, never realizing you can customize.
– Robert Brault

1. Being Who You Are

Let's start work on your soul story. The first step is to work out who you are. Once you've got that, you can work on who you want to be. After all, you're the author of your script and you play the main character. If you want to make the most of your life, you have to make the best of yourself. So let's start at the very beginning. As the song goes, it's a very good place to start.

You are who you are today because of a whole mixture of things. Your background, the opportunities you had, the choices that you made along the way. If you want to make a sustainable change, it's important to know all these factors. You might not like them, but they are the foundation of your identity. You stand a much better chance of changing them if you acknowledge them first. Then you can incorporate appropriate modifications into your plans.

This means that you have to start by knowing yourself. This is an ancient piece of wisdom. The Delphi oracle advised, 'Gnothi sauton', 'know thyself', and Plato quotes this maxim in his dialogues. In Buddhism, to 'know oneself' is the first and last step of human enquiry. For modern psychoanalysts, knowing oneself is the ultimate purpose of therapy. All these traditions share the belief that the external world is ephemeral and illusory: the only thing you can be sure about is you.

And if you do become acquainted with yourself, you'll be much more tolerant of your own foibles. When you truly understand anyone, you can see the world from their perspective. Even people you don't like become much more sympathetic when you see where they're coming from. As the saying goes, before you judge anyone, walk a mile in their shoes. The same is true for yourself: stop judging and practise acceptance. You might start to feel almost self indulgent.

Know yourself, and you'll be kinder to yourself. There may

be things you still want to change, but you'll start from a position of understanding. And to truly understand someone – in an accepting, respectful, non-judgemental way – is a precondition to loving them. This is important, because you have to love yourself before you can give love to anyone else. Who you are now is a unique and special being. You shouldn't dismiss this, and you can't even if you wanted to. Everything in your story so far is part of who you are now. There is a lovely quote about this:

> For men and women are not only themselves; they are also the region in which they were born, the games they played as children, the old wives' tales they overheard, the schools they attended, the sports they followed, the poets they read, and the God they believed in. It is all these things that have made them what they are, and these are the things that you can't come to know by hearsay, you can only know them if you have lived them. You can only know them if you are them.
> – Somerset Maugham, *The Razor's Edge*

So your current self contains all your experiences so far. Depending on your attitude, that's either a limiting thought or incredibly empowering. You were shaped by circumstances outside your control; but you can choose what situations to seek out in the future. Even more importantly, you can choose how to respond to whatever the world throws at you. If life gives you lemons, you can make lemonade... or tarte au citron or mojitos or whatever takes your fancy.

Your past contains the things that shaped you; it doesn't determine who you are now. Equally, there's no point in waiting for a fantasy future. You need to get on with living in the present, which is where your self actually operates. If you want to be happy in the future, you better practise being happy right here, right now. The mind needs stretching and exercising like a muscle. When you regularly channel your thoughts and energies into an aware, interested, enthusiastic state this outlook becomes a habit.

One way to acknowledge the good in your life is to express gratitude. In practical terms, this means showing appreciation for all the things you might take for granted. Express thankfulness to the people in your world – friends, colleagues, strangers in the street. It only takes you a few moments, and it might change someone's day.

"Thank you for clearing up last night, I was exhausted and it was so nice to have a clean kitchen this morning."

"Thanks for getting the report distributed so quickly, I appreciate that you had to work late."

"What a beautiful garden! It really brightens up the road."

Expressing gratitude will also make you feel much better about life in general. Like karma, little acts of appreciation come back multiplied in terms of feeling good about your life. The very fact that you're reading this book means that 85% of the world's population would be deeply grateful for your personal circumstances. When you practise being thankful, this attitude becomes a mental habit. And gratitude for what you've got is a good basis for the next stage of your soul story.

It's a good idea to train your brain by practising presence and appreciation. Here are five things to do each morning so that you start the day in a positive frame of mind.

Activity: Morning Ritual

1. Welcome this brand new day. Wake up, stretch and inhabit this moment completely. Feel the warmth of your covers; smell the scent of your body; see the sunlight playing outside your window. Live completely in this presence. Whatever happened before is over: each sunrise is a chance to start again. Recognize this truth, acknowledge it and start living now. 'Morning has broken like the first morning; blackbird has spoken like the first bird.'

2. Identify something you're grateful for. Express this to yourself before you get out of bed. Be aware of how that thankfulness affects you immediately. Focus on how you can show gratitude through specific action. You can set this the night before to start your morning: "I'm grateful for my health, and I'm going for a run first thing." "I'm grateful for my children, and I'm going to cook pancakes for breakfast."

3. Check your plans for the day. Ask yourself three things: Are they in line with my core values? How will they make the world a better place? What will I remember about today? The first Chancellor of Oxford University, Edmund of Abingdon, gave his students a wonderful precept: 'Study as if you were to live forever; live as if you were to die tomorrow.' If this was your last day on earth, would you still want to do this? Are your activities today supporting your real priorities? What could you include that would give a greater sense of meaning?

4. Follow your own morning routine. Showering, dressing, eating breakfast – these things don't involve big decisions. Morning routines free you to focus on the moment. Enjoy the hot water, feel the fresh cotton, smell the coffee. By being relaxed and present, you set the tone for your day ahead.

5. Give yourself a little inspiration! Some small input that sets you up for the morning. The Internet is a great source – maybe you could sign up for a 'quote of the day'. Other people read self-help books or scripture daily. I have a diary with sayings that make me smile. Boost your self by starting the day with something new.

Why Values Matter

Practising gratitude means knowing what's good in your life already. It's acknowledging all the things that have made you who you are today. This is key for understanding your soul story. Where you are now is just where you need to be. You've had exactly the right experiences to take the next step. When you recognize this, you validate your story so far. This empowers you to become the best possible version of yourself. After all, living the life you want begins with being someone who would live that way. And the key to working out who you want to be is looking at your guiding principles. A good starting point is to identify your core values.

Having values is fundamental to who you are as a human being. Your inner ideals shape how you interact with the world. Every day, you'll make countless decisions on the basis of what you believe is worthwhile. These decisions translate into a series of actions which affect how you relate with everything around you. Each action may seem small, but together they form the sum totality of who you are.

It might not seem fair, but other people judge you on your actions. Not just the big ones that you'd like them to remember. Celebrities give millions to charity but that doesn't mean you'd necessarily want to spend time with them. What makes people feel safe with you is the small things that show kindness. You pick up a snail that's crossing the pavement. You help a young mother carry her pram down the steps. These little acts are indicators to your friends that you would look after them. They are what make people feel safe in your presence.

If everything you do reflects who you are, what about when your actions seem contradictory? Well, maybe that shows that sometimes you're confused. That's quite natural, because we live in a changing world with contradictory aspects. How can you tell whether that homeless person is a feckless druggie or a hero hitting hard times?

Another confusing element is that maybe people you admire had different viewpoints. You can probably still hear these opposing voices in your head. Perhaps you had great respect for your parents, but were also deeply influenced by an inspiring teacher at school. One voice tells you that we're all responsible for making our own way in life. Another reminds you that noblesse oblige, it's right and kind to help those less fortunate than ourselves. Yet another chips in that society has it all wrong: to each according to his need, from each according to his ability. You hesitate, go back and put some change in the homeless man's hat, then feel like a fool… it wasn't enough to buy a coffee, half a loaf is worse than no bread… was that the 'right' thing to do… you try and justify yourself to invisible interlocutors and end up wishing you hadn't given anything.

What you need to do here is work out your core values. This lets you make a plan that you can generally stick with. When someone paws at you asking for money, it's easier to stay calm if you've worked out what you'll do. You don't have to articulate this – that might lead to an argument – but it will stop you getting flustered or self-reproachful. 'I give money to buskers, not beggars, because at least they are trying to offer something in return.' 'I support a soup kitchen because that way I know my money is going on food, not beer.'

Of course, rules are made to be broken! I had a very memorable encounter when I was travelling around India. I'd been visiting the Taj Mahal and was sitting on the train in Agra. Suddenly there was a tapping on the window: outside stood yet another beggar. Impatiently I waved him away. I was a seasoned traveller, not likely to fall for harassment. When I looked up again, I was annoyed to see him still there: but he wasn't begging now. Instead, he was doing a perfect impression of a blasé hippy dismissing a poor mendicant. He mimicked each expression and gesture perfectly. I was laughing so much that it was hard to lean out and hand him money as the train pulled away.

So having guidelines in place like this doesn't preclude you being spontaneous when the occasion demands. If your heart tells you to act a certain way, then just do it! But it does mean that you don't have to work out every situation on a case-by-case basis. Defining your core values lets you make some judgements in advance, as default choices. And that, in turn, frees you for more important decisions.

There's another benefit to clarifying your core values: by focussing on what you believe, you separate out logic from feelings. This means that you can work out what you really want, without being distracted by emotion. Neuroscience shows that when you engage your 'thinking' brain – the prefrontal cortex – you channel your mental resources. The amygdala, the part of your brain associated with emotions, stops working overtime. This means that when you concentrate on analysis, you're not at the mercy of your feelings.

If this sounds familiar, it's because focussed thought is very close to mindfulness. And as we know, mindfulness is just another way of being present in the moment. When you hold your attention on a particular situation, you experience it more fully. This in turn lets you identify an appropriate reaction. So next time you feel disturbed by a situation, direct your mind to control your emotional response.

To do this, start by naming what you're experiencing. Labelling your feelings engages your mind and stops those emotions taking control. This is just a passing phenomenon, you don't need to identify with it. Next, map the current situation in terms of your core values. (We'll work on identifying those core values soon.) Identify which core values are being affirmed and which are being challenged. This lets you plan your response in terms of what you really believe is important. After you've done these first two steps, you're in a position to act. Now, you'll be sure that your behaviour reflects your true beliefs and priorities.

Does this mean you shouldn't set any store by emotions? That feelings are a dangerous distraction from the real stuff of life? Of course not! Thoughts reflect our mind; feelings are the language of the soul. Remember that we are tripart beings: mind, body and soul must all be in balance, if we are to thrive. The body is the physical aspect of our existence. It is very important, because as we have seen, our actions express our inner essence. We are really not just human beings but human doings. The mind is the control centre, the component that can be mimicked by 'artificial intelligence'. But the part that makes you truly human is the soul.

It is your soul that gives you emotions and the capacity to engage deeply with another person. It is your soul that makes you literally humane, expressing your fullest humanity. When you honour the expressions of the soul, your life is enhanced immeasurably. You experience a sense of meaning and purpose, a heightened appreciation of existence, a deeper awareness of life. As you work on your core values, bear in mind that they have a practical application. Your values are the guiding principles which let you navigate the world. You are developing the compass of your soul story.

So take care that your values consider both principles and feelings. To make the most of existence, you have to 'live by the sun, love by the moon.' Of course you have to function in the external world. You must go to work, interact with other people, make decisions based on logical analysis of the situation. This is your daytime persona: practical, pragmatic, efficient. But if you apply the same rules to your personal life, you're cutting out your soul. To experience passion you must be willing to surrender to emotion. In matters of the heart, the moon must eclipse the sun.

Activity: Identifying Core Values

There are several different dimensions that you need to consider when working out what you truly believe. You'll find some key ones here; they may not all seem like moral values, but they are all key determinants of how you see the world. Maybe the most important axis is the one in the last box, which is blank. This is where you can fill in anything else that really matters to you. It might be the touchstone of who you are.

For each of the axes below, mark with an 'X' on the line where you are. Do this quickly, based on your instinctive reaction. It's a subjective response, and there are no right or wrong answers. The purpose is simply to know yourself.

I would say that I am:

Private	Outgoing
Cautious	Daring
Responsible	Free spirit
Optimist	Realist
Generous	Economical
Reserved	Direct, outspoken
Self preserving	Focussed on others
Family first	Friends focussed
Individualist	Community minded
Political activist	Hippy anarchist
Intellectual	Artistic
Creative	Practical
Left wing	Right wing
Religious	Atheist

Now, take a piece of paper and get ready for some writing. For each axis above, give an example of when you've acted in a way that demonstrates these values. It can be a trivial incident or a major life decision. How did you feel about this event afterwards? If you have several that you want to think about, write down as many as you like. If you can recall a time when your actions didn't reflect your values, write that down too. It might be difficult but it will give you some deep insights. Think about how you felt and what you could have done differently. Gather as many stories as you can: these will tell you a lot about yourself.

Finally, it's time to look forwards. Think of a situation that you are likely to face in the near future. This might be a repeat of one of the incidents you've written about; alternatively it could be a brand new circumstance. It might be dealing with something at work, handling a request from a friend, or dealing with that ubiquitous beggar. Write a detailed description of how you'd like to handle it, bearing in mind the core values that you want to express. Telling a story in this way can feel like really experiencing the event. It can be helpful to use the present tense, to make your experience more immediate.

Practising the expression of your core values like this prepares you for new, unseen circumstances in the future. You'll find that with practice, your automatic responses become more and more in line with what you believe.

This above all: to thine own self be true
And it will follow, as the day the night
You can not then be false to any man.
– William Shakespeare, *Hamlet*

Forming Your Self Image

Now you have a pretty clear idea of your core values. You've identified the factors that are important to you. You've practised projecting them into a future situation, to see how you'll respond. The next step is to use this information to form a clear and consistent self image.

First of all, are you happy with these core values? As we've seen, they may not all be under your conscious control. Some of the things you 'think' may be old voices echoing in your head: parents, teachers and other authority figures; the opinions of an older sibling or a friend you really admired. Those people were important in your life, but they were only human. They were operating on the information available to them at the time, based on their own experiences. It might initially feel like betrayal, but there's nothing wrong in questioning these beliefs. If you asked those people today, they might well have changed their position. The world is very different now to when you were growing up. Now that you're independent, it's appropriate to re-examine those inbuilt beliefs.

Your next step is to work out who you want to be. Once more, the place to start is here and now. Once you have a pretty clear idea of your base values, you can move towards being the person you want to be. This person will incorporate all the attitudes and aspects that are most important to you. They will live out all your key values in real life. They will be a suitable hero/ine for your soul story.

That doesn't mean that you have to throw away all that's good in your current life. Say you've decided that you really want to make the world a better place: you want to make some lasting impact. You don't have to give up the day job in order to express this reality. Instead, you could consider volunteering at a hostel one evening a week. You'll meet people with similar priorities to you, and you'll have something new to talk about. This might lead to all sorts of interesting encounters and opportunities.

Let your mind go to work on this. Don't focus on it too hard: lots of the best ideas come from a sort of peripheral mental vision. Soul insights of this sort are rather shy creatures. You can formulate a plan, but then leave it unsupervised for a while. During this time, your mind can play and make friends with all sorts of other wild ideas. When you come back to your original concept, you'll see what has accumulated around it. Most likely there will be thoughts and possibilities that you'd never consciously contemplated.

The main thing at this point now is to flex your mind. Expand your thoughts to include new possibilities, novel ways of seeing and being and doing. Broadening your view of what's possible opens up channels of mental energy. This simple shift of perspective lets different ideas flow into your subconscious mind. From here, they will work their way up to consciousness, taking clearer shape as they arise. And once you become aware of an idea, you are free to catch it – consider it – and act upon it. Purely by envisaging a new way of being, you create potential in your life.

It's time for some practical work. Let's start with a visualization exercise. Don't worry if you're not used to imagework: you can 'picture' an abstract form or even a feeling if no clear image comes to mind. It's hard to remember details for this exercise, so you might like to work with a friend. Alternatively record the instructions and play them back as you visualize: remember to read slowly, and you can stop the recording at any time.

Visualization and visionwork let you gain profound insights by accessing the wisdom of the unconscious mind. The main distinction between them is that visualization draws on what you already know; visionwork lets you imagine things you've never actually experienced.

Your first step is to calm the mind by deeply relaxing the

body. This makes your brain produce theta waves, halfway between conscious waking and deep sleep. In this state you're in a semi-trance, able to blend imagination and reality. You can access information which is held below conscious awareness. William James, the father of American psychology, called this the treasury of the subconscious mind.

Find a place where you can sit comfortably, with your head supported. Some people like to lie down, but I find sometimes the deep relaxation sends me to sleep! You should be warm and comfortable: put on thick socks if necessary. Don't allow any interruptions: remember to switch off your phone. If there is anything on your mind, jot it down on a notepad before you start. That way, you can really concentrate on the present moment.

Activity: Inviting an Image

Relax. Close your eyes. Focus on the feeling. Let your body sink into the seat. Start with your toes. Let them relax completely. Now your feet... let them go completely... feel how soft and heavy they are. Let that relaxation rise up through your ankles... your calf muscles... your knees, your thighs... Release your legs completely. Feel how soft and heavy they are. Now take your focus up through your buttocks, your belly, your chest. Let your arms drop, completely relaxed, dark and warm. Let go of your shoulders, your neck, your head. Let your mouth go loose... your eyes relax...

Your body is soft and heavy. You're totally relaxed. There's nothing to distract you. Any sounds outside anchor you in the present moment. Your body is completely relaxed. Your mind is in a state of deep awareness.

This is here. This is now. Relax deeply.

Focus on yourself as you are now. Invite an image of this to come into your mind. It may be a figure, an animal or plant, even an object. Accept the first thing that comes into your mind. Don't try to rationalize or judge it. This image symbolizes you as you are now.

Examine the image closely. What do you notice about it? What are its qualities? Its strengths? Its vulnerabilities? How do you feel about this?

Now, release the first image and let it drift away. Open your awareness to your core values. Focus on what you want to be like. Feel the power of your beliefs. Invite another image into your consciousness. This image represents your future self.

Examine this new image closely. Take as much time as you want. Are you pleased with this image? Is it how you want to be? If yes, then let the picture expand in your mind. If not, then let the picture dissolve. Invite an alternative image to form in your mind. You can change the vision. You are in control of what you foresee.

When you are ready, bring this picture closer. Study the image in detail. What do you notice about it? What are its qualities? Its strengths? Its vulnerabilities?

Allow yourself to merge with the image. Experience how it feels to be this way. Stay here for a while in silence. Feel yourself present in this image. Accept any insights this experience has to offer.

This image is you when you are in line with your core values. You can 'anchor' this image so that you can reach it whenever you want. Choose a simple gesture – maybe touch your thumb and your little finger. Focus on the new image while you do this. This gesture is a private key to carry with you. Use it whenever you want to remind yourself of how it feels to be this image.

When you have finished, move back out of the picture. Know that you can access it whenever you need it. Release the image and let it float away. Bring your attention back to the feeling of your body. Slowly become aware of the world around you. Hear the noises of everyday life. Feel your body in contact with your chair. When you are ready, open your eyes. As you come back to the present, remember the insights of your vision.

Activity: Drawing It Out

Whilst the image is still clear in your mind, it is a good idea to capture what you saw. The best way to do this is by drawing. It doesn't matter how good you are at art, what matters is keeping the essence of what you saw. Take a big piece of paper – A4 size is ideal – and sketch what you remember. Use coloured crayons to enhance your artwork. Add words, objects and any other accessories that are true to the spirit of your vision. Draw in a background if that would be appropriate.

Keep your picture somewhere you can see it often. Maybe beside your bed or inside your wardrobe door. It will be a private reminder to your self of who you're going to be.

2. Where You're Going

You've worked on who you are. That's fundamental to your soul story. You're the author and the central character. Now it's time to get some idea of where you're going.

Being here on earth is a wonderful opportunity. But a wonderful opportunity to do what, exactly? There are so many options in life, it's hard to know which to choose. Besides, all the really interesting options seem to involve hard work and a lot of luck. That all sounds very serious and it probably wouldn't work out. It might be safer not to try: at least then no-one can laugh at you.

Some people are lucky: right from the start, they see life as play. For them, the world is a giant theme park; they just have to choose their rides. Will they go on a roller-coaster adventure, or sit in the family area watching their children play? Ride a roundabout, doing the same thing over and over; or try their hand at laser quest, going for the high score to beat all their friends? If that's you, you're fortunate – though you need to focus your energies if you want to succeed.

If you take yourself more seriously, then you won't feel quite so carefree. Unless you have a vocation, like medicine, it's hard to know where to start. Choosing what to do with your life seems very definitive. Do you know what you want to do when you grow up? The trick here is to let go, trust to luck, and let your intuition play its part. It's not so important that you make the right choice, as that you get on with something. Open up to the world and see what fate brings you. A chance encounter or casual conversation can show a path you'd never thought of. It doesn't have to be perfect, it just has to be right for you. Perhaps it's time to let go of the controls and dream a little.

Activity: Clarifying the Details

To get anywhere in life, it really helps to know where you're going. So your first step should be to clarify your vision. Hold on – do I hear you saying that you don't know what you want? The trick here is not to be too specific. If you try to work out every detail in advance, you'll almost definitely fail. Best to have a general picture and let life take care of the specifics.

Alright, we're going to put some of this into practice. Think back to those core values that you examined earlier on. Think about how those might manifest in real terms. Some of the questions you might ask yourself are:

- Would I prefer to live in the city? in a village? in the countryside?
- Do I want a job where I save the planet and help other people?
- Or is it more important for me to make a fair amount of money?
- Do I want adventure in my life or do I like routines and security?
- Do I prefer big social events or small gatherings of close friends?
- Do I want to buy a house or might I invest in other ways?
- Do I want a nice car, meals out and designer clothes?
- Or supper with friends and save my money for travel?
- Would I like to live abroad or in my home country?
- Is it important for me to do creative stuff each week?
- Do I need to do sports and get outdoors regularly?
- At what moments do I tend to feel happiest?
- Does it matter for me to have family around?
- Is my relationship a priority in future plans?
- Do I want to have children? a dog? ...

As you think about these questions, you'll find a clearer picture of your future path emerging. You may not yet know all the details but you're starting to form a congruent sense of where the path might lead.

Activity: Feeling the Dream

Now it's time to call on the power of your subconscious. Because when you have put the foundations in place, and unleashed your imagination, then castles really can get built overnight. (That's one of the things that fairy tales were talking about.) We'll be doing a visionwork exercise, this one with immediate practical results.

Visioning lets you access the wisdom of the unconscious mind. It lets you picture what could be, without the inhibitions of logical thought. Your first step is to calm the mind by deeply relaxing the body. This creates a semi-trance, able to blend imagination and reality. You might like to use the relaxation technique from the activity 'Inviting an Image'. Remember, you can record these instructions and play them back to deepen your concentration.

Find a comfortable place to sit where you won't be disturbed. Make sure that you're warm and that the room is quiet. Close your eyes and let yourself relax. Take a deep breath and exhale, long and slowly. Empty your mind of everything. If any thoughts arise, just acknowledge them and let them go.

Feel a soft heat rising from the soles of your feet. Let it travel up your legs, through your body, along your arms to the tips of your fingers. Take another deep breath and exhale fully. Release the muscles in your shoulders and your neck. Let your face relax, your cheeks and jaw. Smooth the lines around your mouth, the creases at the corners of your eyes. Your mind is blank and empty. Your body is soft, warm, heavy. Feel yourself sinking into the chair, totally relaxed.

Imagine that you're in a cinema waiting for the film to start. Become aware of yourself sitting there. This is you as you are now, today. Think of all the good things in your life. Feel gratitude for everything that's gone well so far.

Now the film is about to begin. You gaze up at the big screen and a picture appears. It's you… it's you in five years' time. Study the film intensely. Where are you? What are you doing? What are you wearing? Who else is in the scene? What are they doing there?

Do you like what you see? If you feel uncomfortable, change the details until it feels right. You are the director, you can have whatever you want in your film. Do this until you're completely happy with what you see. Then sit back, relax and enjoy the scene.

As you watch the film, the screen gets bigger and bigger until the picture is all around you. Now you're inside this future world. Become intensely aware of everything around you. All your senses are involved. See the bright colours in your future world. Listen to the sounds around you. If anyone is talking, note what they say. Feel the clothes on your skin. If there is food, taste it. Smell the air…

You're slipping back out of the picture into your seat. Release the film on the screen for now. It's out of sight now but you know it's there. Be aware that this is coming to you soon. Feel an intense sense of anticipation. Relish the excitement.

Revisit this picture whenever you need inspiration. Good times to do this are when you first wake up and just before you go to sleep. When you're feeling relaxed, your mind will be able to recreate the vision. Recall the details: how things looked, smelt, sounded. Each time you repeat the visioning, you're reinforcing new connections in your brain. You're teaching your subconscious to recognize this new place.

Once you have this vision, you can start to create it in the external world. Remember how it felt to be that person. Remember what you needed in that place. What must you do to reach that situation? Every day, take small steps towards your future being. Start moving those pieces into your current life.

You'll find that you are living the dream sooner than you thought was possible.

Help from the Future

Do you ever ask friends for help? Some people are better at this than others. By help, I mean anything from a car share home to a phone call at four in the morning. Of course, some people take things too far. There's a definite line between asking for help and taking advantage. And no-one wants to be the sort of needy, depressive person who pulls others down. But sometimes, opening up can be the best thing to do. By admitting that you're not self-sufficient, you open up the door to some new input.

I know all about this, because it's one of my own issues. For years, I was really bad at letting people help me. I felt that having problems was a sign of weakness: I had to soldier on sorting out my own challenges. I'd make my children walk a mile to the swimming pool rather than be indebted to anyone. I didn't confide in friends or family about personal issues. I'm an anthropologist by training and by nature: great at listening, able to keep a secret, but not very good at talking about myself. It took a really dark time in my life before I could open up to others. Then I found out what a huge relief it was to admit my vulnerabilities. Turns out nobody judged me and lots of other people had similar issues after all.

The problem with sharing your problems is that friends want to help. They come up with solutions that are well meant and much appreciated. It's very hard not to be influenced by such caring advice. But these answers may not be the right ones for you to grow and develop. Your friends by definition are part of your past and your present. They're advising you as the person you are now. They can't possibly know the person you may become.

In fact, there's only one person who may know how things turn out. That someone is possibly the last person you'd ask for advice. It's yourself... or rather, yourself as you turn out to be. Your future self inhabits the place you're heading for. They are the only person who can tell you how it feels, or what you did to get there. So it might be a very good idea to get their opinion.

Does this future self actually exist? You might feel sceptical about this idea. We're taught to view time as having a linear trajectory. There's the past, which contains things that have already happened. This determines the present, which is what you're experiencing now. Then there's the future, which is unknown because we haven't got there yet. It's because the past is gone and the future is uncertain that it's so important to appreciate now.

In one sense this is true. The present is all that we can be sure about. It's vital that you live with 'presence', enjoying all the good things in your present existence. But many traditions tell us that time is an illusion, a convenient way of bundling our experience into manageable blocks. Actually you are more than just a physical entity moving forwards through time. You are a spiritual being inhabiting a physical body which changes over the years; you exist now and then and will be, simultaneously. You are merely focussing your consciousness on a particular time in order to experience it more fully.

Your future self is as 'real' as your past existence. You know that your memories affect how you see yourself. You remember choices and situations, and these explain how you reached the place where you are today. Looking back at the past enables you to make sense of the present. In a similar way, your future self can help you to understand where you are going. By looking back from the future, you can see how to take the next steps on your life path.

The exercise below is a very powerful way of accessing this inner wisdom. You can memorize the guidance, or you may wish to record it for yourself. As you follow these instructions, be aware that you can pause at any time. Take as much space as you need to fully explore this encounter.

Activity: Meeting Your Future Self

Find a chair where you feel comfortable. It's important that you stay alert for this experience, so I'd suggest you don't lie down. Close your eyes and relax. Feel your feet firmly on the floor. Let any tension in your body drain down into the ground. Gradually your body feels lighter and lighter. All around you is a gentle radiance. Become aware of the colour of this radiance. Become aware that you're floating through space and time.

Gradually the light around you changes colour. You're moving towards another place, ten years from now. The light around you settles like mist clearing. Sense this new place taking form around you. See the landscape, the sky, the trees, the houses in clear detail. There is a building ahead of you. What does it look like? You go towards it.

The door opens and someone is standing there. Their face is as familiar as your face in the mirror but older, wiser. You know this is your future self. How are they standing? What clothes are they wearing? They are smiling at you, welcoming you inside. You step in and look around the room. What furniture is there? What colours are the furnishings? What other things are in the room?

You sit down with your future self and gaze at each other. They are smiling at you kindly, compassionately. They remember how it feels to be who you are now. With an open gesture, your future self invites you to speak. You can ask anything you like.

Greet this figure and express your appreciation for this chance. Ask them how they got to this place. What happened to bring them here? What did they do to make this happen? Is there anything else they would like to tell you?

Some questions you might ask are:

• Where are we?

- Why did you come here?
- What was your key decision?
- What work might you do now?
- How do you spend a typical day?
- What are your favourite things to do?
- Who else is significant currently in your life?
- What did you do about... How do you feel about ...
- So what was the first thing you did ... and after that ...
- Is there anything else I should know ...

After each question, pause to let your future self reply. Some of their answers will be clear; other times, give them space to explain fully. Because they have already overcome your problems, everything will be in perspective. They will be able to tell you the first steps, but other things will only emerge as you experience them.

When you have learnt enough, thank your future self for their insights. Stand up together and walk to the door. At the entrance, embrace each other. Feel your bodies blend into one translucent being. Step away and become separate again. The light coalesces around you. Feel yourself lift off the ground into the radiance. You're moving through space and time back towards the present moment.

As you come out of this meditation, be aware that you are one with your future self. You are an integrated whole, a single being who exists outside of time but has chosen to focus on a given moment in order to experience it more fully. This focus allows you to experience the sensation of growth and change.

Bring the insights of your future self back to your current situation. You may want to write them down; you should certainly hold them in your mind when making choices in your life. This perspective will help you to get where you should be going, to be true to your highest potential. You have been given a road map rather than detailed instructions: the way ahead will become clear as you progress.

Note: As you move towards becoming your future self, you may experience a spiritual 'jet lag'. This happens when you have a profound insight and feel you have changed, but still sometimes lapse back into old patterns of thought and behaviour. It's as though you haven't yet caught up with your new self. This happens because it takes time for changes of internal perception to manifest consistently in external reality. Lessons learnt in personal development take a while to become default behaviours. It's just like when we travel through different time zones: the body takes a while to catch up. This is compounded when other people don't recognize your new 'self' and continue to treat you in the old manner. Don't worry: so long as you can hold onto your insight, your new self will come more and more clearly into focus.

Making It Real

We've looked at who you are and worked on where you're going. Now it's time to turn that vision into reality. This is the manifestation of your soul story in real life. It's when you start to see your dreams becoming true.

Making your dreams manifest is both very simple and quite difficult. Simple, because it's a straightforward process. Difficult, because it involves consistent work over a long period of time. A lot of this work is invisible or involves tiny changes. Until things start to show, it's hard to sustain the effort.

The most important thing is to have faith in your dream. This involves what my old English teacher used to call 'a willing suspension of disbelief'. You must convince yourself that this vision of the future is not only desirable, but possible. That it's a realistic and achievable ambition. That although it's a change of direction, it's perfectly congruent with your trajectory. Most of all, that small steps in the right direction will be cumulative.

This last point is very important. You can't expect things to change instantaneously. So you have to believe that small steps add up to something significant. That each move in the right direction is incremental. That every effort you put in will be worthwhile.

What you need to remember here is that you're manipulating energy. Everything in the manifest world is made of energy. This book may seem solid, but you're actually holding an empty block with tiny electrons whizzing around. The chair that you sit on, the drink on that table, the street outside – all of these are literally material constructs. High energy physicists say that the world isn't even a stable illusion: the presence of an observer affects the way subatomic particles behave.

Mass and energy are intrinsically related. Physical objects are made of space with a few charged particles inside. And ever since Einstein, we've accepted that space and time are interconnected: if an astronaut travelled at the speed of light he'd age more slowly. It's hard to comprehend because it's so antithetical to our lived experience. But mass, time, distance – the things that constitute 'reality' – are all aspects of how energy manifests in this physical world.

Rationally you know this to be true. Applying it in your life is another matter. The materially constructed world is so convenient. It lets you predict, manipulate, move things around. It gives you a reassuring sense of stability. It lets you experience change in manageable chunks. But every so often, light shines through the cracks. You experience events which are outside this logical causal existence.

Think back on your life: when have things happened outside the causal spectrum of explanation? You've probably experienced déjà vu: the feeling that this has happened before. Then those times when you thought of someone right before they contacted you. Or you take a different road to work, and later find there was an accident on your usual route. Premonitions and intuitions which turned out to be right. Synchronicities which were just too strong to be coincidence. I've had numerous experiences like this. It's not that unusual, everyone will have some similar incidents. The more you acknowledge them, the more they seem to occur. It's as though the force likes being recognized.

Such experiences remind you of the basic principle of manifestation. All that befalls you is a result of your thoughts. You can choose to take this literally or symbolically: believe that what you think of appears, or that your thoughts determine your actions. The world doesn't really care either way. It's just happy to manifest whatever you choose to think.

What matters is that you start to take this into account. The future is coming whether you're ready for it or not. If you don't plan the life you want, you'll spend just as much time leading a life you don't want. You can decide what should happen, and you can work towards it. Each small change is a move in the right direction. You won't be able to see everything along the way. Sometimes the path will end up somewhere completely different. But taking those first steps is entirely under your control. Starting work on your dream is just a decision. Making it manifest is simply a matter of commitment.

Activity: Chart the Territory

We've said that core values are the compass of your soul story. When you're working out your direction, it helps to know where you want to go. But if you overthink, you'll end up going in circles. Let's be a little playful as we map out the new territory.

Take a large sheet of paper: A3 size is ideal. You'll need some coloured crayons too. What we're working on here is a map of your world.

Think about those wonderful medieval navigation charts. You're making something beautiful as well as practical. Let your imagination run free, to create a picture that will inspire you.

Start close to home, with the world as you know it. Begin in the left corner of the page. Draw a little house to show where you live. Put in the place where you work. Add anything else that is important in your current life. Label things so you can remember what they are.

Now start to think about your future. Move to another part of the paper. Using a different colour, draw your ideal home. Add some scenery around it. Put in more details: Where will you work, play, exercise? What will you need? How will you travel?

Draw little figures to represent the important people in your life. Will they be near your old home or elsewhere? Do you need to add anything for them?

Think about the dangers on your journey. Draw small monsters or danger signs. Olden-day navigators believed that if you went too far, you'd fall off the edge of the world. Label the unknown perils: 'Here be dragons...'

Make your chart as colourful and detailed as possible. Smear around your old house with a used teabag – this gives it an authentic weathered look. Make notes, set symbols, use highlighter. When your map is finished, put it up where you can see it. Over the next few days, add anything else which occurs to you.

Fantasy mapping is a great way of making a world real. Think of Tolkien and those detailed maps of Middle Earth: cartography was a key part of his creative writing. We'll talk more about it in Part III of this book. Having a chart for your new life is a powerful way of developing your soul story.

Invoking the Mind

We've spoken a lot about your soul story. Now it's time to relate this to real life. I want to enlist one of your greatest tools for manifestation. This is the power of thought or more specifically mental imagery. To harness this, you'll need to understand how the mind works.

What are you doing right now? Pause for a moment and focus on what you're actually experiencing. Become aware of your body posture, the book you're holding, the seat pressing against your legs. Feel whether you're hot or cold; sense the rise and fall of your chest as you breathe.

Your body has been experiencing these things all along, but you were unaware of them. You were totally focussed on these words, black lines and curves on a white background. Somehow your brain took these shapes and turned them into images and ideas. My thoughts and concepts, typed into a laptop, are spontaneously reassembling themselves in your mind.

Your body is the interface with the outside world. You experience it through your senses – sight, sound, smell, taste and touch. This data is transmitted to your brain which constructs a model of external reality. But our senses are limited so the data conveyed is in coded form. This system restricts how much information you can get about the external world. The model in your brain is a simplified representation of reality. It is interpreted by a system of awareness which you experience as your 'self'.

What is this 'self' which you experience? You're aware that

it is not just your body. This physical incarnation is something that you inhabit, that enables you to interface with the world. You can enjoy existence, increase your fitness, savour sensation and sensuality. Still, you refer to it objectively: 'my body' not 'me body'. So there must be another level on which your 'self' exists. Your spiritual being is your soul, the part of you which connects to the energies of the cosmos. The third aspect of self, which mediates with your soul and your physical incarnation, is your mind.

For many people, mind is the distinguishing feature of the human species. Hamlet puts it well in his great soliloquy: 'What a piece of work is man! How noble in reason, how infinite in faculty!' The prince is quite unequivocal here: it is our mental powers which he admires primarily. The ability to reason – to exist outside the here and now, to analyse a situation and conceive a hypothetical alternative – is the mark of our superiority to the rest of the animal kingdom. But Hamlet comes to a sticky end through overthinking. Paralyzed by indecision, he ends up destroying everyone around him. To avoid a similar fate, you have to understand the structure of the mind.

The key thing to remember is that your mind has two parts: the conscious and the subconscious. You'll probably be very familiar with your conscious mind. It's the part that you learned to use in school; that you deliberately engage in specific tasks; that lets you label what you're feeling. Your conscious mind is extremely useful. Like a computer, it's full of facts with loads of processing ability. You can store incoming data and even install new programs if you want. But remember, it's not operating alone.

Underlying your conscious thoughts is your subconscious mind. This is full of data too, but it's not information that you selected. What fills your subconscious is a mass of data that you inherited. You're aware that your mind affects your body. When you're stressed or distressed, this can manifest as physical dis-ease. What you may be less aware of is the power that your subconscious has over your conscious mind.

These two parts of your mind are designed to work together. The world bombards your brain with information. All the time, your senses are collecting data: conversations around you, music in a bar, advertisements on billboards, the radio as you drive. Luckily you're not aware of it all, because your subconscious filters it. This leaves your conscious mind free for high-level processing. You only become aware of what's necessary for survival and achieving your goals. But your subconscious mind still has to deal with all that information.

Your subconscious mind doesn't make judgements. It doesn't discriminate between what's helpful and what's not. So if it gets repeated messages, it may start to believe them. You may never consciously realize what's happening: it's what advertisers call subliminal programming. The problem comes when your subconscious starts to apply these ideas. It creates a set of rules which affect your responses. So your emotions and your behaviour are partly dictated by these unconscious laws.

Let's look at the relationship between mind and body more closely. When you were born, you arrived with a full complement of genes from both parents. Your DNA determined how you looked as a child. As you grew up, lifestyle choices began to play a part. Diet, sunshine, exercise – all these factors affect your skin and body shape. What's more, your habitual expressions leave line marks. By their fiftieth birthday, most people get the face they deserve.

Your genes operate at a deeper level too. Conventional science claims that DNA is destiny: your predisposition to certain illnesses – diabetes, cancer, heart conditions – is inherited. But new studies show that things aren't so simple. What actually matters is how you respond to your environment. And this is something that you can alter. So when studies show that things run in the family, what is actually inherited is family culture.

Sure, you get a particular set of genes, but you can choose the circumstances which turn them on or off.

This new science is called epigenetics. 'Epi' is a Greek prefix meaning 'over': other factors can operate over and above your genes, to determine their physical manifestation. This is great news, because it means that biology isn't destiny. You can make choices which override your genetic heritage. You can stop smoking, wear sunscreen, eat organic – program your body to a different physical manifestation. Your mind, acting through conscious decisions, has determined your physical condition.

This is one way your thoughts manifest in the external world. It's a two-way process, of course: your physical condition affects your emotional state. When you exercise, your body releases endorphins which produce a sense of well-being. Conversely, in wintertime, lack of daylight causes Seasonal Affective Disorder (SAD). It's very real – lots of people find that a full spectrum light actually reverses this condition. So we know that the mind and body influence each other. Well, there's a parallel process going on within your brain. It concerns the interaction between the conscious and unconscious parts of your mind.

Let's go back in time and space to when you were a baby. When you arrive in the world, your mind is a clean page. Over the next few weeks, you absorb information through your senses at a tremendous rate. All this data tells you about the world that you now inhabit. Very soon, you adjust to the environment where you live. If you hear English, you begin to babble with English noises; if it's Mandarin, you start to speak with different sounds. As you grow older, you observe how people around you speak and act. You internalize the beliefs and habits of your family: this is how people like us think and speak and behave.

So what are the contents of your subconscious mind? It's a jumble of things which you're probably not even aware of. In particular, it contains a set of rules to filter out what gets through to your conscious mind. Most of these were stored there before you reached the age of seven. These things were initially useful: beliefs and habits which helped you to survive in the world. That's why you were pre-programmed to store them. But in a rapidly changing world, they are probably less helpful.

These unconscious beliefs and habits are what Bob Proctor refers to as 'paradigms'. They can relate to all sorts of things in your life. Most of them start with local generalizations: 'In our family, we always...' 'People like us don't...' Many of your beliefs passed from one generation to the next, as part of your family heritage. Paradigms are programmes which were once relevant but you haven't examined for a while. They are difficult to access because you're probably not really aware of them. But since you're no longer a young child, they may have become problematic. In fact, they probably stop you from reaching your full potential.

The real problem with these beliefs is that change is uncomfortable. We resist examining them because it's painful to do so. Ancient Sanskrit teachings call them 'samskara': mental imprints based on past experience. They exist as cycles of energy and don't cause any problems so long as you don't disturb them. When something triggers one of these suppressed cycles, it releases a surge of energy. You'll feel this repressed association as a blockage in your chest.

If the paradigms are unconscious, how can you change them? The first stage is to become aware of them. The litmus paper here is your comfort zone. If something feels easy, it's probably in line with your dominant paradigms. That means that it won't really change anything in your world: if you keep doing the same things, you'll keep getting the same results. If it feels challenging, or scary, or downright impossible – then you're probably up against a big one: 'People like me just don't...' Once you're aware of this, ask yourself – why not? You'll likely find that the answer is just 'because'. That's a good indicator that you should move onto the next stage. The way you've always been isn't the only way to live. If you really want to change how you operate in the world, start by challenging your paradigms.

Once you do this, the subconscious becomes your ally. Instead of a dictator, it acts as a curator: a source of tremendous riches. The Otherworld is full of treasures when you approach it properly. That's why every hero's story involves a descent into darkness before they can vanquish the monster. That's why the Roman name for the lord of the underworld was Pluto, meaning wealth. That's why William James, the father of American psychology, stated that 'the power to move the world is in your subconscious mind'.

The second stage to changing your paradigms is to involve your conscious mind. This is the rational thinking part of your brain. Logic often gets a bad press in personal development, but here it's your ally. Your subconscious mind is a cybernetic system. Like a guided missile, it locks into a pre-determined program. It detects and automatically corrects any deviation from this target. Your conscious mind, on the other hand, has the ability to select thoughts. When you enrol the consciousness to impress new goals on the subconscious, you can choose to change direction.

Think hard about what you really want to do with your life. It's a truism but time will pass anyway. If you don't plan what you want, you're going to spend your days doing things you didn't want. It seems like a good idea to invest some time in setting your course. Without clearly defined goals, you'll become so devoted to daily trivia that ultimately you'll be a slave to routine. Shift from living by your paradigms to living in accordance with your deepest dreams and desires. You've got one chance to do everything you've ever wanted to do. Act accordingly!

Moving to Manifest

So far, you've been mainly operating inside your own head. Visionwork is manipulating tiny pulses of electrical energy that travel down neurons to create thinking. These thoughts manifest as brain activity which can be seen with electromagnetic resonance scanning. And this process works on higher levels too. Remember that everything is made of energy. What you've been doing on a micro scale, you can magnify. Your thoughts resonate with the world outside. What you can hold in your mind, you can hold in your hand. Anything you can think, can be manifest in external reality. The real fun begins when you start to play with higher energies.

Is this brain activity objectively measurable? Quite simply, yes: it can be detected with scans. Electrical impulses can be recorded by attaching electrodes to the head (creating an EEG or electroencephalogram). EEG is mainly used to study epilepsy. But can this electrical activity be detected at a distance? Yes – dogs are famously able to tell if their owner is about to have an epileptic fit. Sharks have sensors which detect electrical energy produced by the muscles of their prey. Electric eels are the ultimate example of directed electrical impulses. There is no doubt that energy produced within a body manifests in the world outside.

What does this mean for you? It's so simple that it's hard to believe. The truth is that you can affect reality. You can create whatever you want. You can determine your own destiny. All you have to do is maintain a deep and abiding intention. That will evoke the future that you desire.

Of course, it's not quite that simple. The world is a complex system: other people around you are creating their own realities, and sometimes their destinies interact with yours. Add the fact that you start with a huge handicap in the form of unconscious paradigms. And you need to be flexible: I'm not advocating headstrong perfectionism. Sometimes your goals show up in deep disguise. Myths and fairy tales remind us of this profound truth. Beauty has to love her beast before he turns into a prince; Jack Giantkiller swaps his cow for a single bean – though it does turn out to be magic. So manifesting your dreams may not be as straightforward as it sounds. Nevertheless, the truth is that you can have anything you truly want. If it can be imagined, it can be manifest.

If this all sounds daunting, the good news is that the results are predictable. There is a direct correlation between how hard you try and what you'll achieve. There is no shortcut, no secret, no unfair advantage. You simply need commitment to your personal development. It's back to the adage of the Delphic oracle: know thyself. What matters here is mental discipline. You need to practise self-control to realign your mental constructs. It's a matter of using willpower to establish new thought patterns.

It's time to put these principles into action. There's a simple three-stage process to turn your deepest dreams into practical plans.

Activity: From Fantasy to Action

i) Setting Goals

What excites you, thrills you, motivates you? These are the things that you should be pursuing with all your passion. Take a blank sheet of paper, and start to mind map. Write down everything you can think of: dreams and hopes, wishes and aspirations. Decorate and doodle while you think of more. Draw rings and loops and fancy borders. Put little figures marching around your page.

There are probably a couple of things on your page which really intrigue you. They may be odd, individual, idiosyncratic; they might seem a little crazy. Focus on these, no matter how unlikely they sound. If they make your heart beat faster, they are the ones in line with your true story. Take a clean sheet of paper and write one of these dreams in the centre. Around it, write down things associated with this. For example, say you've always wanted to learn horseriding. Write down anything connected with this vision: Black Beauty, ponytrekking as a child, the smell of leather. Draw pictures – horses cantering, you sitting on a horse. Set a verbal goal statement: 'In one year, I will be a competent rider.'

Finally, enlist your conscious mind to retrain your unconscious. Stick pictures of your dream where you'll see them every day: on the fridge, in your car, on your desk. Write your goal statement on a postcard and keep it in your pocket: read it each day. Maybe you can link this with some activity – say, each time you get a cup of coffee. Use words, images, anything you can think of to reinforce the image of your goal.

What you're doing is using repetition to establish a new paradigm. As you've seen, your subconscious mind is very receptive. By exposing yourself to these stimuli, you're establishing a new automatic response. When you program goals in this way, you convince yourself that they could happen.

That's how you make a dream come true.

ii) From Idea to Theory

You've taken a dream and turned it into a goal. This can give you valuable feedback. How do you feel about your goal? Is it exciting, intriguing, creeping into the edges of your waking thoughts? Do you identify on a deep level with this new self image? Or do you feel that it's all rather silly, that you couldn't actually do this in real life? If it's the latter, then you need to go back to step 1 and picture your goal in more detail. Involve your other senses – smell, taste, touch. Make this fantasy feel as real as possible. That's the best way to convince your subconscious mind that it might really happen.

Now it's time to enlist your conscious mind, and move onto the next stage of manifestation. You need to turn your fantasy into a true possibility. This is actually quite simple, and draws on skills you already have from daily life. The key here is a word, which is very effective at initializing your brain power. That word is 'If...'

Find a place where you won't be disturbed for about half an hour. Choose somewhere you feel safe and comfortable. Take a clean sheet of paper and write your goal in just a few words at the top. You've got the dream: how would this goal actually manifest? You're going to see if this is really practical.

Now, write your first 'If...' about halfway down the page, followed by your goal statement. 'If in one year I'll be a competent rider... Then – what do I need to do?'

Your first 'Then...' statement becomes the basis for your next 'If...' You can put this above or below your first statement, whichever seems best. Add a 'Then...' and use this in turn to build another 'If...' Only stop when you reach a practical action point. Then go back up your list to any division points and take them down until they reach practical actions too.

For example, 'If in one year I'll be a competent rider, then I need to start riding regularly.' 'If I need to start riding regularly, then I must find a stable.' 'If I need to find a stable, then I could Google it.' This is a practical action point so stop here. Go back up the list and develop your 'If...' statements: 'If I start riding regularly, then I should get some jodhpurs.' This is another practical action point.

When you've covered everything that seems important, sit back and read through your list. You'll have a series of sentences which show clearly how your dream can become reality. More importantly, you'll have a number of practical things to do. Underline the action points so that they stand out. Some of them will be things you can do now; others will depend on how things work out. Put a star next to the ones that you could do straight away. Pick three that sound quite simple and highlight them. If there aren't any that look easy, go back to doing more 'If... then...'.

You know what comes next. You've got three days – no cheating! Don't go on to the next step until you've done these tasks. This will let you know if your fantasy is really feasible: if you can truly make your dream manifest.

iii) Plotting the Path

So you've set a goal which makes your heart sing. When you think about it, you get a little pulse of excitement. You've turned thought into theory, identifying a series of practical steps. Looking into things more seriously, you've found out that this really would be possible. The third step is to make your dream come true. It's time to build a practical plan.

The trick here is not to make a to-do list. You know the sort of thing, action points and target timeframes. That just means you can change the date and postpone indefinitely. Instead, let's be playful to enlist the power of the subconscious mind.

You're going to draw a story path. This is a critical line which takes you from where you are to where you want to be. Along the way you're going to encounter challenges and opportunities. Some of them lie actually on the road: these are the key steps which you need to take in order. This sequence of stages which you must go through is what project planners call the 'critical path'. For example, you have to lay the foundations of a house before you can start building the walls. Other things are important but can be done in a different order. The furniture for your new house can be ordered any time, but you might like to choose it before you actually move in.

Take a large sheet of card – you can buy them in pastel colours from stationery shops. You'll also need an assortment of coloured crayons. Across the centre, draw a long wavy line. Make the waves big – this gives you more room to write things down. It also reminds you that there will be good and bad times along the way. At the left-hand end of your line, draw a figure to represent yourself now. At the right-hand end, draw a figure to show you having achieved your dream. Along the bottom of the page, write out your goal statement – 'In six months, I will be living in Paris.' At the top, sketch a very rough timeline.

At the moment your path looks quite clear. It's time to put in some of your theory. Take the piece of paper with your 'If… then…' exercise. You've marked the action points so that they stand out. Start with the ones that you've done already. Choose colours to show how you felt about doing them. Write them down near the start of your story path. Now you can see where you are already. Your story is starting to become real.

Now, looking carefully at your story path, decide where the other action points should go. Write them onto your story path in pencil. Space out what you write so there is plenty of room to add things later. The activities on your critical path have to go in the right order. If you need to move things around, it's easy to rub them out and rearrange them. Other activities which are more flexible can go above or below the line. You might choose to group them in some way – for example, above the line for phone calls, below for actual meetings. Illustrate the tasks with signs, diagrams and drawings. Use space and graphics to make your path look interesting.

Now you've got an interactive action plan. Put it somewhere that you'll see it every day. All that's left is to put your plan into effect. If you use a diary, allocate the next few action points to actual days. Remember to add a task of 'Schedule more action points'! Each time you complete a task, mark it in colour. You can choose colours that show how you felt after doing this – red for danger, blue for calm, green for go-ahead...

As you work along your story path, you're turning fantasy into reality. You've begun in the realm of the spirit, playing with the dreams that make your soul sing. You've moved to the domain of the mind, analysing a dream as a theoretical possibility. You've arrived in external reality, changing theory into a practical action plan. Step by step, you can make dreams come true.

Some Thoughts

Your mind must do the work here. Your problem is that you've trained it to be analytical. Logically operating, it might be a bit sceptical about some of these ideas. Just to convince your mind, here are a few quotes from great thinkers:

> If a person will advance confidently in the direction of their dream and endeavour to live the life they have imagined, they will meet with success unexpected in common hours.
> – Henry David Thoreau

> All that you behold, though it appears without, it is within, in your imagination, of which this world of mortality is but a shadow.
> – William Blake, 'Jerusalem'

> We plan our lives according to a dream that comes in childhood, and we find that life alters our plans. And yet, at the end, we can see that our dream was our fate. It's just that providence had other ideas as to how we would get there. Destiny planned another route.
> – Ben Okri

> There are two ways to live your life. One is as though nothing is a miracle. The other is as though everything is.
> – Albert Einstein

3. Telling Your Story

Your life is a story. You're the author and you play the central part. You've selected the setting, chosen your role and allocated the main characters. Every day, you're taking your part in this story. So why do you sometimes feel that you're not in control? That's because you haven't focussed on one key element. You may have literally lost the plot.

Time is the great storyteller. When you look back, you know how things turned out. You see how one event led to another. That's because we experience time as a linear process. Your life story looks like a chain of cause and effect.

But your story also operates on another level. In a deep sense, your life is a manifestation of your soul's purpose. If you want to live your life fully, it's vital that you acknowledge this. Time tells the tale, but you can be a part of that process. This means you can do more than dream about what happens next. You can plan, and put theory into action. You can take control of your life.

What's happened so far can't be changed. It's fixed in time, a part of your life story. What you can change is the relationship of that past to future elements. Because you can decide what will happen next in your life. You can make the story all make sense now. Your soul story operates across time and space. It is the template which gives meaning to your life.

What you'll learn later in this section is how to craft your story. First, let's look at why stories are such powerful tools.

The Power of Words

In the beginning was the word. It's a belief common to many traditions: Biblical, Egyptian, Ancient Sumerian... At the start of time there was a vibration, and this gave rise to sound. Energy transformed into matter: the universe was formed. Everything arose from that first reverberation. Ancient myth and modern science agree here. It's not very different to the big bang theory.

Thus everything started with a word. This is no abstract metaphor: words are fundamental to our existence. Speech is the distinguishing capacity of humankind. To this day, words have the power to shape reality. In a courtroom, they pronounce formal guilt or innocence. In the Catholic church, they provide remission of sins. Laws, treaties, marriage vows – they all have the power to transform existence.

Belief in the power of words permeates our culture. For the Celts, speech was the highest faculty. They held verbal eloquence in higher esteem than brute strength, not least because it increases with age. Ogmios, the god of speech, was held as the origin of everything. A Gallic depiction shows an old man leading a group of enchanted followers with a gold chain from his tongue to their ears. The ability to use words effectively was the special attribute of druids and poets – 'the gifted people'. Spells and invocations were held to change reality. Satires were especially feared, since ridicule brought dishonour and shame. The Irish *Book of Invasions* records how the bard Cairbre sang an invective against King Bres. The tyrant's face broke out in blotches and since the sovereign must be unblemished, he lost his throne.

It's no exaggeration to say that words make magic. This belief is the origin of our term 'spell-ing'. The invocation 'Abracadabra' actually comes from the Aramaic (pre-Hebrew) phrase 'Avra kehdabra': this means literally 'I will create as I speak'. The very word 'magic' derives from the Greek 'magos', a wise man, a worker in words.

Words have the power to change the world. Like most things, they are stronger when they work together. They build sentences, speeches, stories. They can persuade and convince and make you change your mind. They can link facts and form causal chains of events.

They let you tell your own life story.

Stories and Therapy

People love to tell their stories: it gives them a chance to make meaning of their world. Anthropologist Charlotte Linde heard many life stories in her work on narrative and memory. She notes how much energy people put into crafting a narrative that has coherence. To shape a life story, there must be two factors: continuity (what is it about me that stays the same) and causality (what has happened to me that explains the changes). Understanding these factors requires some self-knowledge.

Your personal story is unique, but it will probably follow a fairly common pattern. The blueprint for this path is the 'hero's journey'. This is the universal story described so well by mythologist Joseph Campbell. The hero must leave home; pass threshold tests; travel through the underworld; and return with a boon for the world. They must face monsters, real or metaphorical, in order to prove their worth. Luckily they have a mentor who helps them at the start of the journey. This help may take the form of advice, training or some special gift.

The hero's journey is a cycle which can be repeated indefinitely. At its simplest, it recounts a single adventure: St George meets a dragon, slays it and saves the town. On a more complex level, it forms the basis for many novels and films: James Bond encounters a series of villainous traps before finally meeting the evil mastermind. At its deepest, it represents the difficulties that we must all encounter as we journey through life. Only by passing through the dark underworld of the soul can we experience personal growth.

So how is this process reflected in your own story? Psychologist Carl Jung said that the first half of life is rightly devoted to living: work, play and procreation. In this period, you accumulate things – education, skills, material possessions. Compare these to what the hero gets at the start of their journey. You get a degree, buy a house, collect books or clothes or sports equipment. You're busy setting goals and pursuing dreams. You're concerned with climbing, achieving, performing: working actively to establish your identity.

During your late forties, your priorities start to change. You move into the second half of your lifetime. Now you make mistakes, experience disappointments, acknowledge failures. You learn to accept that things are often outside your control. But this isn't as depressing as it sounds: it's all part of your personal journey. At this point you start a deeper process, which Jung called 'individuation'. As you mature, you focus more on your inner development. Like summer leads to harvest, this life stage brings its own rewards.

The process of self-realization requires deep insight. One way to achieve this is by structured personal reflection. Psychoanalysis helps you identify repeated negative patterns in your life. Self-examination is precipitated by problems, setbacks, difficult experiences. You face your darkest thoughts and dirtiest secrets. In return, you'll hopefully achieve profound psychological illumination.

Such insights don't necessarily need years of therapy. They can result from personal work – introspection, meditation, guided visualization. Sometimes they come from sudden shocks – the slings and arrows of outrageous fortune, as Shakespeare said. You may forfeit something precious as the price of knowledge. You're fired, and your sense of self-worth goes with the job. You fall ill, and realize you can no longer rely on your body. You lose someone, and are left with a dark hole in your life. Father Richard Rohr, a Franciscan monk, calls these things spiritual stepping stones.

It's when you experience such things that you become conscious of your soul's calling. The surface events of your story don't make sense. What happened is unpredictable, unreasonable, unfair. Why did you have to go through such distress? What had you done, that you deserved to suffer? It's all very well trying to cultivate inner wisdom. How can you make sense of what happened? Self-knowledge doesn't nearly answer the question.

Switch off your mind: stop, and listen to the whispers. Logical analysis will take you around in circles. The answers to your questions lie far deeper. The process is not so much learning as recognition. Yes, this is true; yes, this makes sense; yes, this is what I truly want. Your soul will guide you where you're meant to be; in fact, the place where you wanted to go all along. Acknowledge this, don't try to control the process. Following your inner compass lets you integrate mind and soul.

Does this process hurt? Yes, like walking through fire. Your soul is purged like gold being purified. Is it worth the suffering? The answer is not simple. Have you seen Titian's painting *The Flaying of Marsyas*? It's often cited as a metaphor for the pain of artistic creation. It's also a pretty good simile for the process of self-realization. If you have any option, don't start on this journey: stay home by the fire, and be thankful for what you've got. But if there is a drop of wild blood in you – the hero, the traveller, the shaman – you won't have any choice in the matter. Once you're called, there is no turning back.

So what can you learn from this? Your personal narrative is about your journey through the world. It should honour all aspects of your existence. Enjoy your life to the full; keep your body fit and strong; exercise your mind in the realms of the intellect. But above all, seek out circumstances in which your soul can flourish. The inner journey is the ultimate purpose of your time here on earth. Your greatest task is to find insight, purpose and meaning. And that means serious work on your soul story. Socrates famously pronounced that the unexamined life is not worth living. In truth, a life without spiritual awareness is not fully lived.

Why People Use Stories

You are a natural born storyteller. Each day you create stories about yourself. You tell them to explain what's happened to you. You use them to connect with friends and neighbours. The stories are true, but the content is subjective. By choosing what to include, you decide what is important in your life.

Why do we tell stories? Because they are the most effective way to communicate. Everyone loves a good tale: books, films, simply chatting with friends. Stories show us how one thing led to another. They give us parallel experiences which we can learn from. And they let us picture alternative ways of being. Stories let us 'image-ine' how things could be different. Our stories evolve as we grow and develop; and stories are themselves agents of change.

You spin the experiences of everyday life into your personal story. This tells other people about your life: what has happened to you, and how you felt about it. But there's more to your story than simple re-telling. Your story reflects your past experiences; it also operates like a feedback loop. If you define yourself in a certain way, it determines how you behave. When you change your story, you alter how you'll act in the future. You define yourself through the stories that you inhabit.

But why are stories so powerful? Why is narrative so much more engaging than plain facts? Scientists are telling us what storytellers have always known: we are born for story. You've heard of a Stone Age diet: our ancestors were hunter-gatherers who ate fruit, nuts and some protein (mostly eggs and fish), with very little wheat, sugar or dairy products. We optimize good health when we follow a similar eating pattern today. In the same way, our brains evolved to optimize our chances of survival. Humans learned over millennia to take in important information through stories.

People are hard-wired to learn from experience – the world would be difficult to navigate otherwise! The huge advantage that we have over other species is that we have language. Which means we can share experience through stories. This operates on a very basic level when we swap anecdotes: white tea is good for eczema; that ant has a nasty sting. By exchanging information, we short cut having to learn everything for ourselves. At this level, we're not much more sophisticated than our animal cousins: dogs bark for danger, honeybees waggle at food. But humans are far more complex than that. We're programmed to learn from narrative sequences of events.

Activity: Who Dunnit?

This is a game for a group or party. Everyone writes down a surprising fact about themselves. The papers are folded and put into a hat. Someone picks out one paper to read aloud, and everyone else has to guess who wrote it. As you read out more stories, there is a diminishing number of people left. So it should be easier to guess who wrote each one – but it often isn't. This is a great game because it shows how social perceptions link with your soul story.

Neurology of Storytelling

Why do stories work so well? Psychologists may have the answer. Our brains are programmed to perceive patterns: we see faces in clouds and pictures in ink blots. There's even a word for this process: pareidolia. Our brains evolved to identify patterns as a way of learning from experience. When you touch a hot stove, your hand hurts: you decide not to touch it again. It seems that we are hard-wired to spot such causal sequences of events. And that's another name for a story.

Dr Uri Hasson at Princeton University has found that our brains respond to narrative imagery. When you hear a story, your brain activates as though you were actually experiencing those events. When the hero eats a hot curry, your sensory cortex lights up. When the heroine does a karate kick, your motor cortex fires up too. When you hear a metaphor – 'the cat licked me with a sandpaper tongue' – you can practically feel it. Stories are all about sharing experience: the brains of the storyteller and their audience literally synchronize.

What's more, stories can actually alter our brain chemistry. Dr Paul Zak has shown that when we listen to a story, our bodies release cortisol and oxytocin. Cortisol is the 'stress' hormone, made in the adrenal glands; oxytocin is the 'bonding' hormone, promoting feelings of empathy. As you can imagine, this is a pretty powerful combination.

This research has far-reaching implications. Anything you've experienced, you can let others experience too: or at least, you can get their brains to activate. If you relate events that changed your thinking or your way of life, they get that experience too. Even though it's second-hand, they have the opportunity to learn directly from your adventures. This has an obvious evolutionary advantage. People can share formative experiences and learn from them without the dangers involved in actually being there. It isn't telepathy, but it's nearly as good.

So stories really do let you share experiences and emotions. This is key to the spiritual aspect of your personal tripart development (mind, body and soul). Remember the word 'humane' essentially means 'sympathetic', able to identify with the feelings of another and act accordingly. It's what differentiates people from robots: they can compute and move, but they don't empathize. Sharing stories is actually what makes us 'human' beings.

If stories are so important for communicating with other people, just imagine how effective they are for communicating with ourselves. When you think that one thing led to another, you're forming a causal link in your mind. You're telling yourself that's 'why' it happened.

Stories help you see the key figures and themes in your own life. The best stories are often variants on old tales: the fairy stories and folk tales that you first heard in childhood. These narratives reverberate through your adult life. They provide characters whom you easily recognise, and template situations which you find yourself acting out. Let's see how this works – and how you can use it to develop your own life story.

Universal Themes

Myths and fairy tales are stories that have survived the test of time. Stories survive when they replicate through re-telling, because they are relevant to their audience: they address basic human concerns. These themes are equally relevant to our modern lives. The monsters we fight may be metaphorical, but we can identify with the predicaments of the protagonists. Because they are so compelling, we unconsciously take these stories as templates for our own lives. This will cause problems if the narrative is not appropriate to your situation: in the modern world, a girl can't just hope that her prince will come. But when you know what's happening, you can use the power of narrative to change your personal story.

Activity: Your Favourite Story

The stories that we hear as children are really important. They shape how we see the world; they model our interactions with other people; they become a part of who we are. Because of the way stories work, fiction is just as important as real events.

Think about the stories that you've really loved over the years. Let's spend some time thinking how these have influenced your view of the world. Take a pen and paper, and write down your answers in as much detail as you want.

Let's begin when you were very young.

Once upon a time... What was your favourite fairy tale? Recreate it with as much detail as you can. Who is the main character? What happens to them? How do they survive? What is the best moment?

Now think back to when you were age nine or ten.

What was your favourite book? What is it about? Who are the main characters? Which one do you identify with? What are their main qualities? What happens in the story? How do they cope with this? What are the best moments? What do these show about your favourite character?

So now remember when you're about fifteen...

What was your favourite book? What is the story about? Who are the main characters? Which one do you most identify with? What happens to them? How do they cope with this? What does this show about them? What are your favourite incidents? Why did you choose this book?

Look back over what you've written. Can you see any common threads? Are there any contradictory elements?

Think about your own life. How do you think these stories influenced you? What similarities do you have with those characters? How have those stories affected your outlook? Are there parallels with your own life?

Hold onto these insights, you'll be needing them when it

comes to formulating your own life story.

Common Characters

To tell a story, you obviously need characters. And to make things simpler, you create a cast of characters which are easy for your audience to understand. This means you probably simplify them, just presenting their basic personality traits. To do this, you unconsciously draw on a set of stock figures from stories you have encountered before.

Certain characters appear in stories from around the world: the princess, the trickster, the wise man, the wicked witch... They are based on universal figures which the psychologist Carl Jung called 'archetypes'. These characters are outline forms which everyone recognizes. You visualize their actual appearance on the basis of your personal experience. Your idea of a 'good mother' will be based on your own childhood. Your 'hero' may be inspired by films and news stories. You recognize these figures easily; you also project them onto people in your own life.

Archetypal figures appear in traditional tales and modern ones. 'Cinderella' is the oldest story in the world: she is a princess figure, demure and passive, waiting to be rescued. There is a version from Ancient Egypt called 'The Rose-Red Slipper'. It is the basis for countless books and films, from *The Philadelphia Story* to *Pretty Woman*. By contrast, Scarlett O'Hara in *Gone with the Wind* is a clever girl who can take care of herself. Jack the Giant Killer is a folktale urchin, echoed in characters like Huckleberry Finn or the Artful Dodger. Theseus fighting the Minotaur is a typical Greek hero: active and arrogant, with a tendency to mindless aggression. You might recognize him as Indiana Jones or Mad Max.

There are twelve basic archetypal figures. They are all potentially present in everyone: you'll tend to identify with one or two as your habitual social image.

Archetypal Figures

	Young	Mature	Old
Light	Princess	Good Mother	Grandam
	Noble Youth	Hero/ine	Wise One
Dark	Clever Child	Wild One	Witch
	Urchin	Trickster	Ogre

It is very important to acknowledge all of the archetypes within yourself – including the dark figures which you may be reluctant to identify with. If you don't, they will probably come out at unexpected moments, in uncontrolled ways. This potentially has the power to destroy you. If you're always meek and helpful, other people may take advantage of you: your resentment builds up until you suddenly explode. If you're constantly kind and caring, your friends and family can take you for granted. One day it's just too much: your anger bursts out and shocks everyone, including yourself.

Light and dark do not mean good and evil. Like yin and yang, they are complementary aspects of existence. Both are an important part of you: your willingness to own them determines how effective you are in the world. If you're a woman, you're traditionally supposed to be caring and nurturing. But sometimes you need to be wild, creative and free. Men are meant to act the hero, fixing things and giving up seats. But standing up can lead to being knocked down. Sometimes you could simply step aside and trip your opponent, trickster-style. Suppose you have strong ecological beliefs: it's no use just manifesting wisdom – to save the world, you need to be an ogre with appropriate environmental legislation.

If you're still reluctant to acknowledge the dark side of yourself, think of it this way. A rainbow contains many colours: pure white light is made of every colour combined. In the same way, self-knowledge means recognizing both positive and negative feelings. You might want to be 'good' but to achieve this you must acknowledge that you're capable of every emotion. Only then can you fully understand others and literally experience true 'com-passion'.

It can be equally difficult identifying the 'dark' characters in your soul story. Calling someone a witch or an ogre sounds like a pretty harsh criticism. If the person in question was close to you, this can feel like a betrayal. The trick here is to see them as a human being, not just a character in your story. This lets you view them as a real person, with their own set of flaws and virtues. Say your mother was a wild woman: maybe this gave you a positive role model for enjoying life. Suppose your father was a trickster: he was unreliable, but he had some smart ways of protecting his family.

Conversely, the 'good' archetypes have their own problems. The princess can feel shy; the good mother is too self-sacrificing; the wise man is sanctimonious; the hero is a jerk. When you're identifying archetypal roles in your soul story, try to see the characters clearly for that they are. Once you release any preconceptions you'll find all the archetypes have both strengths and challenges.

Activity: Identifying Characters

Like any good tale, your soul story has a cast of characters. These are the people who are and have been important in your life. Some of them only played a temporary role; others will be there for you whatever happens. What counts isn't the length of contact, but the effect these people had on your life. Even someone whose trajectory only touched yours briefly can have a major impact on your world. When this happens, you'll find traces of their influence echoing down the years. Other people you can see every day for decades, but they never really touch your heart or mind. When you leave that house or job, you don't expect to meet them again. That's how you know if someone is really part of your soul story.

Because soul stories exist in multiple dimensions, organizing your characters is like herding cats. You could list them in order of appearance. You might want to rank them in terms of influence. You could have parallel thematic lists, where some names appear more than once (work and play if you married your boss). Play around with whatever suits you best. This activity gives you one idea.

Take a large piece of paper and divide it into quadrants. Label them like this:

Friends + Interests   Work + Career

Childhood + Family   Significant Meetings

In each quadrant, write the names of people who made a real impression on your life. Don't include anyone just because you ought to. It's not a question of politeness. Only list those who have played an important part in your story. There will probably be 20–50 names in total: any more, and you're listing peripheral people.

Next, use crayons and symbols to allocate each person an archetypal role. Use the list above and invent your own colour scheme. That lets you allocate favourite colours to the people you like best! You could use a crown for the princess, a jester hat for the trickster. Remember that the archetypes are not gender specific. What you're doing here is identifying the parts that people have played.

Finally, look for repeating patterns. Maybe you attract people who need mothering, or find you're drawn to hero types. Have the same characters tended to reappear in your life? Conversely, did the same person play different roles on other occasions?

Take as much time and paper as you need to do this properly. You'll want to play around with names and roles as you work out the characters in your soul story.

Re-telling Your Story

The way other people see you is influenced by the stories you tell. Equally, your self image is a direct result of the stories you tell yourself. The tales you tell affect how you feel, both physically and emotionally. They have a real effect on your body, because you are incarnate – literally, made of flesh. As we've seen, hearing stories actually affects brain chemistry, evoking physical sensation and emotion. Stories work at the level of the mind, body and spirit.

Changing your story is taking something that you do anyway and altering it for your benefit. Let's take a practical example. It's a rainy day, you're running for the bus but it pulls away just as you reach the door. You're sure the driver saw you, why wouldn't he bother to wait? When you arrive in work half an hour late, do you act depressed and victimized – or make up a funny story about the incident? Which will get a better response from colleagues? Which will make you feel better?

Everyone has incidents in their past which they are not happy about. You may have some memories which make you feel guilty or scared. Even if it wasn't your fault, you feel responsible for what happened. As we've seen, your mind automatically tries to make sense of things through a story. Every time you revisit this story, you are reinforcing those links in your brain – even though it is not the only way to interpret events.

Obviously, you can't change what happened at the start of your story – but you can alter how you interpret it. It's often difficult to see the turning points in your life: you are too close to view things objectively. The plot of your own story – how one event led to another – is only evident in retrospect. Changing how you tell your tale affects how you move forwards from here: it lets you make a story with a happy ending. Now that you understand this process, you can modify your personal narrative. You can make your story turn out any way you decide.

If you want to influence a child, don't tell them what to do: give them a story. If you want to change the world, don't make more rules: tell a better story. And if you want to change your life, start with your own story.

Activity: Reframing Your Story

What happens when you want to change your story? There are five simple steps to reframing your narrative. It's probably best to write things down, so that you can see your thoughts clearly.

1. What's your story? Identify a key event or period in your life / career. Where and when did this take place? What actually happened, in detail? Who else was involved?

2. How has this affected you? What message did you take away from that interaction? Do you still believe that message now? How has this affected your choices and behaviour since? How do you feel today about these events and people?

3. Re-cast the players. This is the crux of your new story. Don't change what happened, but choose a new character for yourself. Identify appropriate roles for everyone else – trickster, witch, supporting cast. (Hint: think about archetypal characters interacting.) Some examples might be: Your mother wasn't mean, she was just insecure. That teacher wasn't being kind – he was creepy. The difficult colleague probably felt threatened by your competence. You weren't weak, you were only young: you did well to survive!

4. Tell your story again, but from your new perspective. You're not a victim now, but a trickster or a clever girl. How was this incident part of your life journey? Write it down or film yourself talking. It's important to have a record of your new story. Gather evidence to convince yourself of this stronger role. Evidence might include: Photos that show you having fun. Friends who share memories of good times. Notes from colleagues thanking you for your contribution. Find tangible evidence that will boost your self image and help you feel confident.

5. How will you behave today? Your new character has implications for the future too. If you can, find something iconic to remind you of your new character. Clothes are good: a red jacket, a pair of smart shoes. You've changed the trajectory of your life story. Make sure you keep on your new path through the dark woods.

When you reframe your story, you interpret things quite differently. This is a very empowering process. You've chosen a new character with a fresh path ahead of you. What happens next is a result of that choice.

Structuring Your Story

When I was a child, I used to write stories. I loved writing: creating alternative versions of reality that let me live life in different ways. My first book began when I was about seven. It told the adventures of a small girl and her corncob doll. I continued writing over several years. My characters shared all sorts of exciting experiences, mostly set around where I lived. By the time I was eleven, they were fleeing a war zone (probably inspired by *The Silver Sword*). My writing style had developed considerably, but the characters stayed the same. Whatever hardships were faced, they were brave and loyal, clever and kind. I think maybe they were an expression of my soul story.

Children love fiction: they exist half in a fantasy world. When you're young, life is so full of possibilities. Anything that you could dream, you could become. You could be a pop star or a famous footballer. You'll write best-selling books and travel around the world. What are you going to be when you grow up? Maybe you don't yet know the answer to that question.

As a child, my life was imaginably colourful. I soaked up the world around me – whether that involved external reality or my rich fantasy realm. There was no need to analyse: the world was wealth enough. Then came the teenage years. I move to another country – literally and metaphorically. Suddenly I was surrounded by a peer group who seemed emotionally stunted, brutal, unkind. Externally I learned to hide my feelings and become invisible. For mental relief, I started keeping a journal. When I reread those diaries twenty years later, they were so raw that it was unbearable: I burned them.

Nowadays, I realize that my experience was not so unique. For many people the teenage years are tough. Mean girls only act that way to keep a place on the ladder. Queen bees see challengers circling around the hive. Still, at the time it seemed all-subsuming. Luckily I had my stories to sustain me. I knew that if I was kind and clever, brave and loyal then I'd survive. My inner stories had become a part of my external world.

For a child, fantasy isn't escapism: it's playing with possibilities for the future. This is a wonderful way to approach the world. As we grow older, that unlimited potential starts to drain. Reality closes in around us, dulling our perceptions, undermining our dreams. The people we trust help us put on handcuffs. They mean well, and they can't help it: their paradigms limit their sense of possibilities. Be sensible and go to college. Play safe and get a good job. You tread water, doing the right thing, investing in the future. Each step makes sense at the time. You're setting up a sort of life insurance. Instead of dreaming, you're defending yourself against the world.

I can show you a much better insurance policy. You can still do the sensible things. Study so you have a qualification. Save some money as a buffer against hard times. But alongside these, remember to keep weaving your soul's dreams. The practical steps are like the warp threads of your fabric. You add colour and pattern with your shuttle threads.

By all means work hard, keep fit, buy a house. Do the things which will keep you safe and secure. But at the same time, stay aware of your soul story. Spend time with people who bring out your best self. Go to the places where you feel excited, uplifted, fulfilled. Do things which are congruent with your story. Every day, take baby steps towards your dreams.

So let's start work on your soul story. As with any story, there are three stages: beginning, middle and end.

Beginning: The Story So Far

The first thing to do when crafting your soul story is to see the past clearly. All that has happened to you so far is a part of that narrative. Specifically, it's the story of your life.

Start by writing down your memories. You can do this in two ways: sequentially or randomly. If you want to start at the beginning, I'd suggest you get a beautiful notebook. On the first page, just put your name and address. (If it gets lost, you want this to find its way back to you.) On the third page, draw a family tree. On the fifth page, write the names of all the people who've really influenced your life. It's really helpful to get the characters for your story clearly. Finally, start the actual record: state the facts of the case. 'I was born…'

As you begin to write, the memories will start to flow. It's a good idea to write only on the right-hand side of the book. This lets you go back and add any details or anecdotes that occur to you later. Illustrate your writing with pictures, maps and diagrams. If you'd prefer to record memories as they occur to you, write on loose paper. Keep this in a folder with dividers for different periods of your life.

Record your life right up to this present day. Be as honest as you dare: no-one else needs to see what you've written. Broad outline is enough for now, you can add more details later on.

Activity: Five Friends

It has been said that you are defined by the five people you spend most time with. It's a strange thought, because you may not have actively chosen them. One of them might be the person who sits at the desk beside you. Another could be family – parents or siblings you see most nights. Or a child – and you didn't know how babies come with their own character. Even your friends may be chosen by default: you live or work close by so you end up spending time together.

How does this influence work? It's partly pragmatic: you adopt the opinions and values of those around you in order to fit in with the group. But the influence also works on another plane. Remember that everyone has an energy field. You don't have to be clairvoyant to sense this, though some people can see it radiating as a coloured aura. You can feel this most strongly when you touch, skin to skin. This lets you consciously transfer energy with powerful healing effects, as in therapeutic or sensual massage. Holding hands creates a circuit which operates like a feedback loop. The infinity symbol – like a figure eight on its side – empictures this exchange. Hugging someone lets you cover them with a protective shield. Sexual union can release tantric energies which allow two souls to merge.

The people you spend time with affect you deeply. Some people have a warmth and magnetism which draws you closer. Others always seem to see the dark side of things. What you might not have been aware of is how much these attitudes can rub off on you. It's all very well having heroes like Mandela or Gandhi. If you actually spend most of your time at a kick-boxing club, that's how you'll respond when the mud hits the fan.

So identify the five people who you spend most time with. Be honest here: not the five people you'd like to spend most time with, but the five people you actually do. For each of them in turn, ask yourself:

- Why/when/where do I spend time with them?
- What are their key goals and ambitions?
- What five words best describe them?
- Who are the important people in their life?
- What do they get from our relationship?

Are you happy with your answers? Is there anyone you'd like to spend less time with? Who else could fill that space in your life? How would you answer these questions for them? Is there someone you'd like to spend more time with? What are you going to do about it?

Middle: Where You Are Today

Now you've recorded your story, you're in a good position to reflect on it. Start by assessing what you've written. Does it read like a novel or a series of short stories? Is the overall tone positive or pessimistic? Have you generally achieved what you wanted? What are you especially thankful for? Do you feel satisfied with your life so far?

Next, analyse your present situation. It's helpful to do this using 'wh' words: who, where, what, when, why. Ask yourself questions like: Who do I like having in my life? Why do I like living where I do? What are the best things about my life? Identify what's good and bad about your current position. Recognize that you are responsible for your story. Where you are now is the result of your past choices and actions. That's great news, because it means that you can do something about the next chapter.

Finally, think about the relationship between present and future. Use the same prompt words to draw out your thoughts. Ask yourself questions like: Who do I want to keep in my life? Do I want to stay living where I am now? Why do I feel unhappy about X? When would be a good time to make these changes?

Activity: With A Little Help From My Friends

You can't do everything on your own. Sometimes it's good to get a little inspiration from others.

Choose as many people as you want, from a few close friends to your entire Facebook friend list. Write a short note explaining that you're looking for new ideas. Ask each person if they would be willing to share some things with you. Stick to five, so it's easy for them to reply. If you do this by post, it's a nice touch to include a reply card and stamped envelope. Good things to ask might include:

- One thing you do every day
- What you keep in your handbag
- Your best hint or household tip
- A favourite quote
- Your life motto

End: How It Turns Out

You've already put some work into deciding where your life might go next. Now you need to see how your plans work out. Remember to keep your eyes on the goal, and to keep taking little steps in the right direction. At the same time, you can't see all that the future holds. You need to stay flexible about your route.

If you can see your path laid out in front of you step by step, you know it's not your path. Your own path you make with every step you take. That's why it's your path.
– Joseph Campbell

It's a good idea to start keeping a journal. This lets you record what happens and how you felt about it. That way, when you look back you'll be able to see how far you've come. Choose a nice notebook that will inspire you to use it. Make an appointment with yourself – every day, or once a week – so that you write regularly. Start at the front with what's happened; at the back, record quotes, ideas and anything else that strikes you.

Your soul story isn't just about what happens: it's about the significance of that too. It's a complex pattern that weaves together people, places, experiences and feelings. It gives significance to intuition and acknowledges the gifts of synchronicity. It acknowledges links beyond a simple causal relation of events. Keeping a journal lets you reflect on all these layers of meaning.

The questions below should get you thinking about your life. They start out fun and get more serious. You can do them on your own or with a friend. It's a good way of learning about yourself and bringing you closer to a partner.

Activity: Twenty Questions

1. Which superpower would you like to have?
2. Who would be your dream dinner date?
3. What would constitute a perfect day for you?
4. What is the greatest accomplishment of your life?
5. Which personal quality are you proudest of?
6. What is your most treasured memory?
7. What would you change about your childhood?
8. How is your relationship with your mother?
9. Who is your closest friend? Why did you choose them?
10. What qualities do you rate most highly in a partner?
11. What is your most embarrassing memory?
12. For what in your life do you feel most grateful?
13. If your house caught fire and you could save just one thing, after you'd rescued family and pets, what would it be?
14. When did you last cry? What was it about?
15. When would you say you really grew up?
16. What would you really like to know about the future?
17. If you had one year to live, what would you change about your life?
18. If you were to die now, what would you most regret not having done?
    - why haven't you done it yet?
19. Do you have a premonition about how you'll die?
20. What would you like to be remembered for?

4. Relationships

You've explored your values, found your direction, developed your narrative. Now it's time to look at the others in your world. Relationships are one of the key things that differentiate a soul story from a life narrative. They are the main reason for your physical existence: you're here so you can meet others. Some people come into your life to teach you a lesson; others to keep you company along the way. A few are fellow spirits, born to share this experience with you. If you're very lucky one will be your *anam cara*, your soul partner.

Relationships are fundamental to your time here on earth. From the briefest encounter in the street to the soul connection that lasts a lifetime, you exist in relation to other people. Whether you have a wide network of friends or a few close confidants, your relationships are the physical manifestation of your inner way. In a good relationship, you become the best possible version of yourself.

It's no exaggeration to say that relationships are what make life worthwhile. The whole point of incarnate existence is that you can touch another spirit. Isn't that an amazing concept, that you can actually connect with another being? Physically and mentally, using touch and language, you relate with others following their own paths. You should take every chance to connect with the people who matter in your world. Hermits may choose to meditate in solitude, away from the distractions of the world. For most of us, this would be missing the meaning of life.

When we're born, the world gifts us with a network of relations. This is our first 'don' or gift (from the French word donner, to give). Right away, infants are programmed to respond to a human face. Even two dots above a horizontal line gets their attention. By six weeks the sight of a person evokes a dazzling gummy grin. (This is clever evolutionary programming: their sleep-deprived mothers were about to return them, but these smiles make it all worthwhile.) The extended family network sees to it that the new arrival is incorporated and socialized. Babies who for some reason aren't able to access this support system – war babies sent to an orphanage, for example – spectacularly fail to thrive.

That's not to say that you're defined by these early connections. They are like a starter pack of cards – you can decide which connections to keep in your life. As you grow older, friends and partnerships become increasingly important. There's a maxim that friends are the family you choose for yourself. Of course, friendships are often defined by circumstance: you may socialize with neighbours and colleagues. This makes it even more important to select close friends wisely. We've also heard how you're swayed by the five people you spend most time with. Whether they are upbeat or downbeat, positive or negative, they will affect your sense of possibilities. Be aware of this influence, and choose your companions carefully.

The people who are important in your life are connected with you. Sometimes you'll experience this connection in manifest ways. You'll think of someone and shortly afterwards get an email from them. Once I picked up the phone to call an old friend and she was already on the line – it hadn't yet rung at my end. We can dismiss these events as chance, coincidence... or we may call them insight, intuition. We can live in a world denuded by logic, or we may choose to wonder at the incredible richness of incarnate existence.

Those who are closest to you are connected by a filament thread. This is a bond so light yet strong that it lasts a lifetime, no matter how far apart you are. Oriental wisdom speaks of a 'red thread' which connects you to the people who matter in your life. As you age, it gets shorter so that the people who are meant to be in your life will come closer to you. I love this image of relationships which are meant to manifest during your time here on earth.

The threads which connect you to others form a network of relationships. Your network includes all the people whom you have genuinely touched. I picture this literally as a glowing hammock which supports you safely in this world. This concept was familiar to the Celts, who knew of the 'web of wyrd' which connects all living things. (When Macbeth met the three wyrd sisters on the moor, they were wise women not crazy witches.) Modern chaos theory tells us that a butterfly flapping its wings in India can cause a hurricane in New Orleans: the insights of mythology and modern science are surprisingly similar.

How this communication works is not properly understood. Maybe it is some form of energy which has not yet been identified. Scientific experiments into telepathy and psychokinesis have not been very illuminating. The effects are too subtle to be reliably replicated, but if you've experienced this force you won't doubt its reality. Physicists tell us that when one atom moves, every other atom in the universe moves to realign. The existence of subtle forms of energy seems fairly trite compared to this cosmic shift.

This innate sense of connection probably resonates with your personal experience. You are instinctively drawn to people who will play complementary roles in your life. You walk into a crowded room and identify who you can talk to, make love with, maybe even marry. Apparently chance meetings seem to resonate with some form of psychic energy. Somehow we connect with the people we can truly communicate with. A friend of mine jokingly calls this complementary neuroses: people select partners whose problems dovetail with their own. I'd rather recognize it as a profound spiritual connection. Trust your intuition and you will find your spiritual travelling companions.

We're here on earth for such a brief time. It's imperative that we make the most of this opportunity. Connecting with others is fundamental to the human experience. It strengthens us, enriches us, widens our outlook on the world. Relationships give us a reason for living and let us live for a reason. They are a doorway to something greater than ourselves. At the end of the day, all that matters will be how many lives we touched. Each evening, look in the mirror and ask yourself: 'Did I love? Did I connect? Did I make a difference?' There is no better measure of time well spent.

Physical Touch

Most relationships begin on a physical level. Your first relationship is the mother-child bond. It's a deep connection based on complementary roles. The mother is primed to look after her child; the baby responds to care and attention. Human infants need love even more than they need food. Psychologist Harry Harlow showed that baby monkeys prefer cuddling a terry-cloth 'mother' to a wire frame that provides food. Children raised in orphanages show a similar need for affection. This early experience of connection lays the foundation for loving in later life. Whatever happens, you've known how it feels to love and be cared for.

When you are older, you're ready to form connections with potential partners. These usually start out with physical attraction. You see a face or brush a body, and feel a surge of excitement. You communicate interest by the way you stand. You test the connection by making contact – a touch, a kiss, an embrace. How they respond determines what happens next. Whether it's a one-night stand or a long-term partnership, it all starts with physical touch.

As human beings, we are physical creatures. Scientists may debate the nature of reality, but in everyday life we operate on a practical level. Our experience of the world is mediated by our incarnate existence. At the most basic level, this means that we interpret reality through physical sensation. In other words, we believe what we can feel. Touch is generally considered even more reliable than sight. We may get eighty per cent of our information from vision, but everyone knows about optical illusions. The ultimate test is what you can feel with your fingers, even when your eyes are closed. This is why you can make love in the dark: you feel your partner there, even though you can't see them.

Physical contact is fundamental to your human existence. The best way to make contact with someone is to reach out and touch them. Of course, it's important to respect social propriety. I'm not suggesting that you go around bestowing unwanted affection on people. At best, this could lead to some awkward situations; at worst, it could get you accused of sexual harassment. So judge your interventions carefully.

There are three levels of contact to consider here. Your aim should be to maximize contact at the appropriate level. Anglo-Saxons are notoriously undemonstrative: reach out a little more than usual. When you meet someone, shake hands continental-style. Connect with people who serve you in shops or cafes using smiles and eye contact. Say hello to people you pass every day in the street, even if you don't yet know them. It all shows that you're paying attention, and everyone likes to feel appreciated.

For family and close friends, the rules change – and this is where you probably don't hug enough. People are often quite inhibited when it comes to making physical contact. They focus on feeling self-conscious rather than on what the other person might need. If a friend is sad, put your hand on their arm. If they are celebrating, you'll want to embrace them. You'll quickly sense if your friend isn't comfortable with this type of touch. If so, simply stop – no harm done. On the other hand, you might be surprised how much they appreciate it. Many people have very few opportunities to hug.

Small children are especially good when it comes to expressing affection. They have no qualms about coming to sit in your lap. Whether they like you or need comforting, there are no inhibitions about expressing their feelings. And they are right to expect hugs on demand. Hugging makes you happier: embracing for half a minute gives you a boost of endorphins which literally lift your mood. So when you put your arm around someone's shoulder, you're actually both getting an emotional boost.

With romantic partners, it's even more important to connect through touch. Long-term relationships often become perfunctory: the key is to maintain a bridge of communication. Because we are incarnate beings, the best way to do this is through physical contact. Love matters, but it's not enough to sustain a lasting connection. You have to commit not only to the person but to the relationship itself. This involves work – consideration, cooperation, understanding. It also gives the potential for extraordinary emotional and spiritual personal growth. The commitment in this type of relationship is unconditional. This means you give without expectation, because your priority is your partner's well-being. You don't have to safeguard your own needs because you trust each other totally. You communicate this commitment through loving touch.

Activity: Body Awareness

Imagine you've been given a new car. You look at it with amazed gratitude. Firstly, the colour – what an incredible shade. Then the size – how many doors? Does it have a soft top? Is it a racing car or rather more sedate? Is the interior soft and comfy, or hard and edgy? Are there any features you especially like – inbuilt satnav, quadrophonic speakers? Is it brand new or does the paintwork need touching up? Do you like it how it is, or would you like to make changes?

When you're given an automobile, you appreciate it. You look at it objectively, its good points and its shortcomings. If you want to make any modifications, you plan accordingly. Your body is just another vehicle to get you around in this incarnate world. Why not treat it with the same respect?

Let's take some time to really appreciate your body. We'll run through your body just like we did with the visualization exercise. But this time, instead of obliteration, you're aiming for awareness of presence. You want your brain to produce alpha waves, a calm meditative state. Are you sitting comfortably? Then let's begin.

Start with your toes. If you can see them, look at them carefully – otherwise you'll just have to visualize them. Are your toenails clean and clipped? Curl up your toes, then let them go. Are there any callouses on your feet? Rotate your ankles – do they move easily? Come up to your lower legs. Can you see any veins? Stretch your calf muscles and release them – how does that feel? Bend you knees slightly, then straighten them. Feel your thighs against the chair. Bring your attention up to your buttocks, clench then relax. How is your lower spine feeling? Become aware of your belly, warm and heavy inside. Breathe in deeply and feel your chest expand; let the breath go. Move your arms, clench your fists, wriggle your fingers. Lift your shoulders up then back. Drop your head from side to side. Suck in your cheeks, then relax. Wrinkle your nose, raise your eyebrows. Breathe in deeply once more, then let your whole body relax.

Let yourself sink deeply into your seat. Feel gratitude for all you have just experienced. What a wonderful vehicle your body is! Let feelings of appreciation and thankfulness wash through you. This is what it means to be incarnate. It may not be perfect, but your body is strong, mobile, functional. You are so lucky to be inhabiting it here in this moment.

Decide to stay in awareness of your body for the rest of the day. You might stretch, go for a run, book a yoga class for tomorrow. Maybe you could have a long bath. Rub in body lotion or a rich handcream. Put on something which feels good next to your skin. Make a nest of cushions and put your feet up. Appreciate each of your senses, especially the sensation of touch. Celebrate all the good feelings that your body can bring you.

Meeting Minds

At a primary level, you are an incarnate being. You inhabit a body which enables you to connect with the world. You do this through your senses: seeing, hearing, smelling, tasting and – above all for interpersonal relationships – touch. The five senses can bring you enormous pleasure. They allow you to 'experience' creation: to relate with what is out-side your personal body. Connecting in this way is one of the great joys of incarnate life. It can also bring immense pain. As you grow older, or when you fall ill, your body reminds you not to hold on too tightly. Ultimately you must transcend the body for higher planes of existence.

What is true for you as an individual is multiply true when you connect with others. Relationships are about more than just the physical body. When you touch someone – a friend, a child or a lover – you connect with them on a very basic level. This touch releases a flow of energy between your bodies. Often this is almost imperceptible; you may not even be consciously aware of it. What you may feel is a warmth, a physiological change due to the release of endorphins in the body. This is a rewarding sensation: whatever your relationship with that person, you're likely to feel closer to them and want to touch them again.

When you become aware of that warmth, that's a sign that you've engaged your brain. It's the brain which is responsible for authorizing that release of hormones; it's the brain which labels your response. The heightened energy may be labelled pleasant or unpleasant, exciting or frightening. Physiologically speaking, these states are very similar. You name them on the basis of external stimuli (safe versus dangerous) and past experience (how did this sort of situation turn out before). That's how you decide whether to seek out more, or to back off fast. Walking with wolves could kill you; a funfair ride is probably a safer bet. (Personally, I'd opt for the wolves, but you can choose!)

So far, you're still in react mode. You're responding to stimuli in a very basic way. At this level, you're still acting instinctively. It's a useful mode of operation: it keeps you safe and it lets you make use of previous experience. It's the level that most of the animal kingdom operates on, and it's extremely effective. But it's not going to let you develop new responses very quickly: it's going to keep you trapped at the ground level of operations. When things become interesting is when you become aware of your brain working. This second level of consciousness is what we call your mind.

Being aware of your thoughts is the key characteristic of human experience. It's what differentiates us from animals. According to Descartes, it's how we know that we really exist: "Cogito, ergo sum" (I think, therefore I am). But existing on your own would be pretty lonely. Human beings are born to bond. We've already seen how fundamental touch is to human welfare. In a similar way, your mind has a deep need to connect with other minds.

You've heard of a 'meeting of minds': the phrase implies a connection beyond the ordinary. When you engage your mind, your relationships move onto another level. Teaching children, debating with friends, planning a life with a lover – these things involve a part of you that can't be seen. Your mind is just as important as your body. A 'purely physical' relationship implies a limited connection. To become your best possible self, you need mental compatibility too.

True relationships are ones where you connect in mind as well as body. It's easy to find someone you can have sex with. It's much harder to find a partner who is mentally compatible. Maybe one person in a hundred will match you intellectually; one in a thousand will have similar tastes and interests; one in ten thousand will also share your values and beliefs. When you meet someone whose mind matches yours, you've found something precious. For each of you, this is a rare chance to learn and grow.

When two minds connect, you'll probably be using words. Spoken or written, words are indeed strong magic. They have the power to change how you think. And as we've seen, changing internal reality can transform the external world. The following activity shows how you can use word play to transform your mind.

Activity: Word Games

If you think you don't like it, change the label! This is a good way to deal with someone who annoys you. Take a piece of paper and divide it into three columns. On the left-hand side, list the personality traits that you find difficult. For example:

rude
messy
extravagant
self-centred

These things may drive you crazy, but there are other ways of looking at them. In the next column, write out a good aspect of each quality.

rude	->	honest
messy	->	relaxed
extravagant	->	generous
self-centred	->	self-nurturing

Maybe you could learn from your nemesis. Like homeopathy, their qualities might help you if taken in small amounts. How could you benefit from being more like them? In the last column, write some action plans.

| rude | -> | honest | = | say what you want directly don't expect others to mind-read |
| messy | -> | relaxed | = | stop being so uptight don't sweat the small stuff |

| extravagant | -> | generous | = | give time/thought/money |
| | | | | leave the world a better place |

| self-centred | -> | self-nurturing | = | wear cotton next to your skin |
| | | | | put on your own oxygen mask |

Soul Contact

Before you were born, your soul knew more than you do now. It didn't use words, so it's hard for you to recall. Besides, forgetting was part of the arrangement. You have to experience life first-hand, or you miss the whole point of the experience. But sometimes things remind you, and then you feel recognition. You might sense this as premonition, or instinct, or déjà vu. Just occasionally, you encounter something so big that your world shatters. Everything really strong has been broken: it's how light gets in, through the cracks.

When you first arrived, you knew your soul song. You came to conscience in a woman's womb. Everything around conspired to care for you. Your needs were understood, your wishes granted. Birth was convulsion, but the breast soon followed. You slept and woke again and loved the world.

Inevitably you experienced separation. The time your mother failed to heed your call. You cried again, and soon enough she came. But now the seed of mefiance was sown. You learned that self and other were distinct. Still you existed in a state of wisdom. Experiences poured in through your senses. Everything connected, everything joined up. Your wonder was as deep as your innocence. You greeted the world with a Buddha smile.

Then you learned to speak. Suddenly things were not

continuous after all. The world was divided into different concepts: packets that divided one thing from another. Verbal communication was a struggle; your vocabulary limited what you could express. Controlling your infant body was hard enough. Now you had an operating system without a manual. Small wonder that you focussed on developing body and brain. Your spiritual skills were temporarily sidelined.

Children make soul connections quite spontaneously. Their vivid imaginations bridge the gap between fantasy and the physical world. They take it for granted that they can see fairies. It comes so naturally that they don't bother to practise. Our society doesn't help: in school they study maths and geography, play games and do gym. The curriculum just doesn't cover spiritual development. So when they hit puberty and life gets more complicated, it's not surprising that the soul stuff gets forgotten.

It doesn't have to be like this. In traditional societies, the spirit world was recognized and revered. Among northern tribes, wise men called shamans operated as a cross between priests, medics and social workers. In sub-Saharan Africa, 'witch doctors' could weave a spell or cast a curse. For Australian Aborigines, all senior members of the group were responsible for re-creation through 'dreamtime'. But in post-industrial Europe, spiritual wisdom was sidelined.

For most teenagers, the first time they experience spiritual contact again is through making out. That's when energy sparks between two people. Having sex feels great because orgasm focusses this force like a lightning rod. The sense of fire, of passion, of union creates an electric fusion. Two bodies become one; for a moment you're not alone in the world. Sex is stronger than any drug and just as addictive. Making love is the ultimate expression of soul bonding.

How can you rediscover spiritual connection in adult life? One way is through sexual activity. Some people get their fix from a series of sexual partners. Others commit to mate for life, like swans. Either way, sex is an important part of pair-bonded adult relationships. At its best, sex is a transcendental experience. Making love is the temporary surrender of selfhood in pursuit of higher communion.

Another way to make spiritual contact is with the innocence of childhood. Approach the world with wonder, deliberately opening yourself to new possibilities. If you are non-judgemental, you can meet people with an open heart. This genuine contact opens the possibility for soul communication. The measure of success here is not length of encounter: it takes only a moment for an angel to touch you with their wings. The meeting may only last a few minutes, but in that time your souls can connect.

One of the best ways to release your spiritual energy is to focus on the chakras. This is a Sanskrit name for centres in your body where different types of force are concentrated. There are seven chakras, from the root at the base of your spine to the crown of your head. When you open these centres, energy flows between them. Mind, body and soul connect so you feel refreshed, focussed and empowered. The exercise here focusses your energetic connection with a partner. It can also be used for a personal meditation.

Activity: Spirit Levels

The exercise here is a tantric practice to increase the energetic vibrations between two people. It can be done with a friend or a lover. Wear as little clothing as you're comfortable with. Bare skin facilitates the flow of tantric energy.

The room should be warm and the lighting low, to focus on your connection. Start by kneeling, facing each other. Your knees should be almost touching. Place your hands on your knees. Look into your partner's eyes. Breathe in deeply, filling your lungs and belly; exhale very slowly, synchronizing your breaths. Repeat this five times.

Hold up both hands, palms facing outwards. Place your hands against your partner's so that they are barely touching. Feel energy coursing between them. Maintain eye contact with your partner. Breathe in deeply and exhale very slowly, in time with each other. Repeat five times.

Keep one hand raised, in contact with your partner's hand. If you're with someone of the opposite sex, the man should keep his left hand raised, the woman her right hand.

Place your free hand over your pubis, in front of the root chakra. This is connected with feelings of safety and being securely grounded. Release the energy in this area. Sense the vibration in your partner's body. Keep looking into their eyes. Breathe in deeply and exhale slowly, in time with each other.

Move your hand to your lower belly, over the sacral chakra. This is connected with sexuality and well-being, acceptance and being open to new experiences. Maintain eye contact and breathe deeply, synchronizing energies, as before.

Now place your hand on your solar plexus, slightly above your belly button. This chakra is connected with confidence and feeling in control of your life. If your upright hand is getting tired, lay it palm upwards on your knee. Breathe as before.

Place your hand on your heart, in the centre of your chest.

The heart chakra is connected with love, joy and inner peace. Maintain eye contact and breathe deeply.

Next place your hand on your throat. This chakra is connected with truth, self-expression and purpose.

Then your forehead, the third eye chakra. This is connected with imagination, wisdom and intuition.

Then on your crown, the top of your head. This chakra is connected with spirituality and the experience of pure bliss.

Finally, raise both hands again and place them against your partner's hands so that the palms barely touch. Feel the warmth and vibration between them. Still keeping eye contact, breathe deeply and exhale in synchrony as before.

Place your palms together and make a small bow to thank your partner (namaste).

5. Gifts

Finding Your Gift

Let me start by telling you something nice. You are unique and special. Don't smile wryly and shrug. You may not feel very special. You don't have superpowers. You're often uncertain about the best thing to do. Some days you actually feel quite down. There are times when it feels like you can't go on. But you know what? You do go on. You've never given up completely – or you wouldn't be here today.

The fact that you don't feel extraordinary is to your credit. No-one else has ever had your particular combination of skills, gifts and experiences. No-one else has ever brought what you do to the world. No-one else has ever had your soul story. And if that doesn't make you unique, what does? In one sense you are ordinary – you're one of billions of people on this planet. But you're still the only one of you. That makes you very special – to the people around you, to the universe, to god or however you want to put it.

I want you to really focus on this. When I say you're unique, I'm not just being nice. I'm saying something very profound about the nature of the universe. You respect other people, don't you? You wouldn't deny that anyone else was special? No, of course not, because you're considerate of others. You know that every person counts towards making up the world. So why on earth would you deny this basic respect towards yourself?

Actually there's a very good reason why you might not like the idea. How does it feel to know you're special? You might say it's a warm fuzzy feeling, like being hugged by a sort of cosmic parent. Well, parents do hug you – but not all the time. Usually when they embrace you, it's signalling some sort of separation: setting off for school, leaving on a camping trip. You get the hug to show their love and faith that you'll do well without them. It's a final infusion of energy before you go out into the world: a sort of magic shot to set you up for whatever lies ahead.

Here's the catch about being special. It means that you have to behave that way. I don't mean you should act arrogant all the time. Life would be pretty complicated if everyone went around acting like the special one. It's more a matter of attitude. When life gets challenging, remind yourself that you matter. Straighten your shoulders and stand tall. Stay calm, focussed, self-assured. Treat others with respect and expect the same in return.

So far, so good: but now comes the hard part. You see, this isn't all about you. You're unique, and that means that you have a 'don' – a gift which you bring to the world. And with gifts come responsibilities: you're morally obligated to give back to creation. You have something to give which no-one else can offer. That's a very powerful thought, and it can be quite daunting. Because it comes back to the meaning of life, the very root of your existence. How will you manifest your unique gift?

Of course, you don't need to wait for a drum roll from the skies. One very good way to get good at giving is to practise. Let's look at some of the gifts you can start to give the world.

The Gift of Love

When I was at high school, I wanted to play guitar. In the 1970s, all the coolest people could play guitar. All the best groups – Eagles, Genesis, the Rolling Stones – had brilliant lead guitarists who oozed sex appeal. Joni Mitchell, my musical role model, actually wrote her own songs. Obviously this was a path I was meant to follow.

Luckily a teacher at school had complementary aspirations. He set up a small group where we learned to play tunes using just three chords. It's amazing how many songs you can play using just A, E and D if you're a bit creative with your stringwork.

Beatles, folk, gospel... One of my favourites was *Love Is Something If You Give It Away*. I can still sing it all the way through (it's not very complicated). Love is something if you give it away, you end up having more.

It's a simple lyric, yet a very profound insight. There are countless other truisms along the same lines. It's love that makes the world go round (Gilbert and Sullivan). The greatest thing you'll ever learn is just to love and be loved in return (David Bowie). Love is the only thing you can take with you when you die. At the start and the end of our lives, all we have is love.

Love is the greatest thing, but also the smallest. I'm not just talking about grand love affairs here, though of course they are wonderful. Romeo and Juliet were willing to lose everything for love. When you're young – in years or in heart – it's wonderful to be overwhelmed by passion. But tiny acts of love and kindness really do make life worth living, both for the recipient and the giver.

The best thing about this is that it's a win-win situation. Love really is something if you give it away. It only becomes real at the moment of manifestation. At that point, it crystallizes from a warm fuzzy feeling into something tangible. At its best, 'love' isn't a noun at all: it's a verb, as in 'to love'. Which means that it needs to be manifest to become real. True love is the unconditional acceptance of another person combined with actively prioritizing their well-being. It's only when you behave like this – putting someone else's welfare above your own – that you are truly loving them. Real love manifests purely through caring actions.

This means that true love is by definition unselfish. When you love someone, you put their well-being above your own needs. You want what is best for them, whatever that costs for you. Your behaviour bears this out consistently. Falling in love is the easy part: your actions are the acid test of a relationship. Staying in love isn't a matter of luck, it's a decision by two people that their relationship is worth working for. For real lovers, passion and excitement are complemented by daily acts of kindness and consideration. True love lasts because it's a practical commitment.

Another great example of this is the parental bond. You were too young to remember, but you've already received unconditional love. When you were a baby, your mother would have done anything to keep you safe. If a T-Rex put its head through the door she'd have leapt forwards crying, "Eat me!" That's because new mothers are hostage to their hormones. Later on, the dynamic between parents and children becomes more complex. This is when it takes acts of love to keep the relationship functioning.

How can you show someone that you love them? Focus your intention on doing, not just telling. Make it clear that their welfare is your priority. Always try to see things from their point of view. If you have an option, think what would make them happy. You don't have to guess: often it's easiest just to ask them. Shall I cook supper tonight? Would you like to see that film? Let your actions come from a place of loving kindness. Running a bath, giving a back rub, buying a small gift – these are all ways of letting someone know you care. Far from being airy-fairy, love is a practical action.

The Gift of Attention

For many people, the most precious thing they can receive is the gift of attention. It fulfils a very basic human need. Attention means acknowledging that someone else exists. It validates their existence in the phenomenal world. It recognizes the unique combination of skills and experiences which form their persona. It's a way of bearing witness to their individual soul story.

The simplest thing you can give anyone is a look. Just making eye contact with another person lets them feel acknowledged.

People who feel ignored become clinically depressed. This is why 'sending someone to Coventry' is such dreadful punishment. If you have more time, give someone the gift of your focussed attention. Look them in the eye, listen to what they say, nod at the right places to indicate comprehension. Actively listening to someone in this way affirms their identity and validates them as a human being.

Of course, it doesn't stop there. When you go out, make a conscious decision to smile at someone. Pick the sourest, grumpiest person you can find: they probably need some loving kindness. It might be the first smile they've received all day. The really lovely thing is that it probably won't be the last: smiling is contagious. Thanks to you they'll probably smile at someone else, and get another in return. And it goes without saying that you'll benefit too. There is a simple physical feedback loop operating here. When you smile, you're telling your body that you're happy. Abracadabra, you start to feel better about the world.

The Gift of Service

In Patrick Leigh Fermor's autobiography, *A Time of Gifts*, he describes travelling on foot across Europe. One of the wonderful things about his journey is the hospitality he finds along the way. Everywhere he goes, people receive him with warmth and kindness. The poorest people welcome him with unquestioning generosity. Why would they act like this towards a stranger, someone who will never pay them back? For people who give like this, repayment is not an issue. Sharing reflects their appreciation of common humanity.

The gift of service is how you connect with the world around you. It's strongly connected to the gift of love. The difference is that you give without any chance of reciprocation. The act of service is its own reward: you do it because it makes you feel good about yourself. This is something which comes more easily to some people than others.

A friend told me recently how upset she was with her brother: at their father's funeral, he cornered her and complained that he felt left out. He said this standing in a room full of guests, holding a plate of food cooked by her, without making the slightest move to help. She was flabbergasted: how on earth did he think the event was happening?

You have to stand up and be counted. You must act without waiting to be asked. Of course, not everyone wants to be a leader. That's fine, the world needs plenty of workers too. But you do need to step forwards and join the team. Some people do this instinctively; they tend to be strongly rooted in this incarnate existence. If you are very much in touch with your body, either through sports or yoga, you may be someone who naturally does things which help those around them.

Other people are more academic, interested in sharing ideas. This is wonderful, but you need to complement intellectual affinity with tangible actions. It's all very well having deep thoughts, but remember Maslow's hierarchy of needs. You need to feed the body before you can entertain the mind. Children need meals, students need books, the sick need bandages. I'm a writer, so need to remember this when I surface from a day at the computer!

Similarly if you're extremely spiritual, that's no substitute for actually doing good. You might have good values, but you have to put them into practice. Remember that all scriptures emphasize the importance of charitable work. By all means meditate and pray for world peace: then go out and do something about it.

Train your mind to focus on practical actions which connect you with others. These can be small scale or major impact. What matters is that you convert the good thoughts into actual behaviour. You don't have to embark on a huge project to change the world. One really nice way of reaching out is random acts of kindness. This is when you do little things that will benefit complete strangers. Leave a book on the park bench with a note inside; pay for the next person's cup of coffee; put coins in a parking meter that's about to run out. Create small surprises that will brighten someone's day. You'll never see their faces, but it's a sort of secret santa: it's kind of fun just knowing that you've made the world a nicer place.

Giving and Receiving

When we give to others without expectation of return, we become most fully ourselves. The Japanese have a saying: 'If you see a weed, pick it.' Make this attitude part of your daily interaction with the world. I'm not advocating that you change who you are, simply how you behave. You want to connect with the people around you: acts of service let you have a positive impact on the world. You need to connect with those you love: practical actions show them how much you care. With luck they will be doing the same for you, but that really isn't the point. In this sort of interaction, it's the person who gives that benefits most. That's because by giving to others, you connect more fully with the world outside you – with the rest of the universe.

Opening up to others is the best thing you can do for yourself. If you're feeling tired, or bored, or isolated – it creates those tiny filament bonds that make the fabric of incarnate existence. Simply smiling at someone keeps you connected with the world. Changing your body language to match – open, welcoming – is like opening a door to cosmic energy. When you give someone your full attention, there is an energetic connection between you. Some people can channel this energy more strongly than others. In the past they might have been called witch doctors or shamans. But anyone can feel it if they focus; everyone can benefit from creating this connection.

You are a unique mixture of strengths and skills, thoughts

and ideas. Taken together, they will let you make a meaningful contribution to the world. We've referred to this gift as your 'don', your personal given. It's a blessing, of course: what a wonderful opportunity to make the most of incarnate existence. It's also a huge responsibility. Your don is unique: no-one else can sing your song. If you don't do what you can, that contribution will stay forever hidden. The process of giving and receiving represents your life purpose in this universe.

Your gift is the contribution that you make to the world. In practical terms, it's based on your unique combination of skills and talents. Skills can be acquired; talents are the abilities you're born with. They both need practice to make them useful. Your gift can be used for personal benefit or collective good. It's fine to contribute in return for prosperity: that's called making a livelihood. Equally, you may choose a gift of service without financial reward. It doesn't matter what you get in exchange for your contribution. The important thing is that you give what you can to the world. Matching your gift to your actions gives a feeling of unity or bliss.

Luckily it's easy enough to start. Giving begins with the people around you. Family, friends, community – they all need your gifts. Don't wait to make a grandiose gesture. Give every time you get the opportunity. Leave this world a better place than you found it. Touching other people's lives is practical immortality. That's enough reward to make it all worthwhile.

Your gift is the ultimate expression of your soul story. It allows you to pull everything together: the people you've met, the places you've been, the experiences you've had, the lessons you've learned. When you view the pattern of your life, you see how it all leads you to where you are meant to be. The good times, the hard times, the dark times and the regeneration: it all brought you to where you are meant to be. Your don shows you how the story all made sense after all.

So what is your soul gift to the world?

Part III

We must be willing to give up the life we've planned, so we can live the life that's waiting for us.
– Joseph Campbell

The Way Ahead

Your soul story is a great adventure. It's also the most natural thing you've ever done. It should feel easy, as though you're going with the flow. Something you're not fighting to make happen, but helping to become manifest.

Still, there may be times you feel uncertain. How can you be sure that you're doing the right thing? It's simply a sense of being 'on track': you know that life is going as it should. You recognize that you're on course because of the excitement that you feel.

But actualizing dreams takes mental and physical energy. Even the strongest adventurer can get tired. It takes awhile to integrate your new being into your daily life. You'll need to find a source of inner strength. Luckily there are time-tested practices to help you along the way.

Be conscious of the energy inside you. It doesn't come from food or physical heat. It wells up and fills you from within. When you're exultant, this energy flows through you. It refreshes you, recharges you and radiates from you. If you're depressed, you close your heart so the energy is blocked.

All the great spiritual teachings recognize this energy. In yoga, it's called Shakti; in Chinese medicine, it's called Chi; in the West, it's called Spirit. It's a cosmic force that you can access at any time. To access this energy, note when you feel love and enthusiasm. These are the times when you're being true to your soul's calling.

This power is your source of inner strength. As you relax and open, the force flows through you. You have boundless energy and enthusiasm. You radiate warmth and well-being. You connect with the people around you. You can even affect the health of your body. Knowing how to access it gives you energy for your spiritual practice.

The foundation of spiritual practice is presence. This means simply being in the present moment. Observe what's going on around you. Notice the leaves on the trees, the wind on your cheeks, the sound of a tap running. Connect with the world through all of your senses. As you maintain awareness of the world, you'll feel cosmic energy rising up inside.

Practise meditation every day. This doesn't mean sitting cross-legged with incense sticks, though that's great if it works for you. What I mean is simply being in quietness. Be aware of thoughts flitting across your mind. Don't engage with them. Let yourself be calm and still. This brings your brain into a state of theta wave activity where the two halves of your mind connect. Your conscious and subconscious work together, bringing a deep sense of unity and purpose.

If you have painful thoughts or emotions, let them go. Focussing on them only gives them a stronger hold. Choose to release whatever was worrying you. Relax your shoulders, exhale and let go. Remember mental activity is a form of energy. Don't let this block and choke you up inside. You might feel pain or tightness in your heart. Relax, breathe out and release the energy.

Whenever you can, get outside. See how abundance manifests in nature. Each tree has manifold leaves, each one of them singular. Draw on the Taoist practice of quietism: align yourself with the flow of the natural world. Let go and immerse yourself completely in your surroundings. Allow your senses, mind and body to connect. This is the most natural and intuitive form of enlightenment.

Let things go. Give things away. Release your expectations. Don't try to force the world to go your way. If you're stubborn, life will give you feedback. People or events will let you know what's wrong. Accept the message and move on.

Learn to be positive no matter what happens. Agonizing over things just blocks your energy. Underneath each problem is a question; under each question is an opportunity. Train yourself to see the good in every situation. Recognize that every thing you relinquish leaves space in your life for something new.

Travel light. Clear out your possessions. If you finished with something, pass it on. Don't make your home a shrine for memories. If you live in the past, you'll block the future. This is a basic principle of feng shui. The more space you have in your house, the more freely energies can flow.

Keep your body fit to do your soulwork. Observe how external factors affect you: diet, exercise, getting enough sleep. Notice how you respond to caffeine, alcohol and sugar. You are responsible for this amazing vehicle. Be thankful for your physical existence which lets your spirit experience this world.

Enlist your mind to help you with your practice. Be aware of the power of words. Don't say, "I'll try to"… say "I will". Use your words to set up an intention. Of course it doesn't matter if you miss meditating one day. What does matter is your stated mindset. This makes it much more probable that you'll act that way.

All of these things come together: you're working to align body, mind and spirit. Your practices affect your perceptions, which influence your thoughts, which determine your reality. With time, you'll learn to command your attention so that the world can't hijack it. If it sounds hard, remember that you're doing the work anyway: you're constantly creating your own future. The difference is that now you know your soul song, you're doing it with intent.

Soulwork is not always easy. Some days you're dancing; other times, your heart feels blocked. Learn to recognize that state. Relax your shoulders, breathe out and release the tension. Feel the energy rise up inside you. Let it flow through you, let it flow from you. Let yourself align with your soul story.

Spiritual Awakening

Your soul story isn't just about what's happened in your life. It's about the meaning that you ascribe to those experiences. It's a many-layered pattern that weaves together people and places, events and emotions. It gives significance to synchronicity and meaningful coincidence. It recognizes connections that transcend time and space.

This multi-dimensional perspective acknowledges the power of intuition, premonition and déjà vu. You perceive patterns that have meaning beyond the simple links of cause and effect. You'll start to see the world around you differently. It's like a translucent parallel reality which coexists with this phenomenal plane. Hardly surprising if you find this disconcerting.

What you're going through is a spiritual awakening. It's a process that tears up your roots and leaves you tumbling in flood waters. It can be chaotic and painful, sometimes almost beyond bearing; it's also cleansing and cathartic and leaves you purified with light. We mentioned this briefly before; now let's look at this experience more closely.

Learning your soul story is discovering your true self: your deepest yearning and your reason for living. It can give you boundless energy yet leave you in such darkness you can hardly crawl. It may make you utterly alienated from your current world. At the same time, it will give you a sense of oneness with the universe. These paradoxes are part of the process: a spiritual rebirth which burns away everything which is not good and pure and true.

If this sounds like a tall order, believe me it is. Gnostism, soul wisdom, does not come cheaply. Traditional societies were well aware of this. We know their customs from hunter-gatherer groups like the earlier inhabitants of North America and Australia. For them, spiritual awareness was an everyday practice, linking their activities with the natural world.

Among the northern tribes of Europe and the Arctic, a few individuals heard the spirits calling. They had to leave the group and go into the wilderness. For weeks they survived alone, learning to communicate with the spirit world. The process was difficult and dangerous but they returned transformed. They were revered as shamans: a combination of wise man, doctor and priest. They didn't have a choice about this calling. It was seen as fate, a vocation beyond their control.

Do you have a destiny? Some people seem born to follow a big dream. Gandhi, Mandela, Martin Luther King: these names conjure up great causes. Moses was called to lead the Israelites out of slavery in Egypt. According to the Bible, he got this message from a burning bush. There's a powerful metaphor here: the bush is burning but never consumed. This shows that the source of energy is outside this material world. It is a cosmic force, which some call divine.

In contrast, Forrest Gump thought life was a box of chocolates: you never know which one you're going to get. You'd probably like to be somewhere in between these extremes. You don't want a destiny that's too onerous. On the other hand, it's good to have some meaning in your life. Your destiny is part of your soul story. It's the path that you were born to follow. It expresses your unique gift, your contribution to the world.

Great leaders show that following your soul's call can be dangerous. You might face ostracism, prison, even death. But there's an inevitability about their stories. The commitment was made very early on. Once they had begun, there was no turning back.

Your soulwork starts when you first hear the summons. It would be so much easier to ignore the call. You could shut the door and bar the windows; stoke up the fire and settle down with a drink. But something keeps tugging at your conscious. A small suspicion that all is not quite right. If you ignore it, it will stop eventually. But somewhere in your heart will lurk the saddest words of all: 'What if...' You'll live your days never knowing what might have been.

And if you heed the call? Then life will get a thousand times better. But it might get a thousand times worse first. The old stories warn that you must pass through darkness before you reach the light. It's like the ancient Sanskrit concept of karma in reverse. You have to pay for what you get in life. And some things have to be paid for in advance.

Maybe your world won't undergo a major upheaval. You may stay in the same place, with the same people in your life. Your soul story takes all you've done so far and links that with future experiences. Maybe all it takes will be a small shift in direction. Changing your path by even a few degrees can lead you somewhere quite new.

Still, you'll undertake a process which leaves you stirred and shaken.

When you heed your soul's call, your whole life is altered. Your sense of identity will be transformed. Your relationships will change beyond recognition. And your outlook will shift beyond belief. It's a dangerous process for those around you, as well as for yourself.

None of this makes sense until you start to experience it. By then it's already far too late. Heeding your soul's call isn't really a decision: it's a recognition that the choice has already been made. You'll probably start by getting some of these signs of spiritual awakening.

One of the first signs is a surge of energy. You're suddenly enthused about everything. You feel so high you could almost fly. This energy doesn't require you to eat extra calories. It seems to come from a source outside yourself. It's the same energy that you feel in the tantric exercise on opening the chakras.

You'll need much less sleep than previously. You'll also experience changes in sleep patterns. You may stay up late – life is just too intense to spend time asleep. Then you'll wake in the middle of the night. This is the sleep pattern that most people had before electric lights were invented. You rest for a few hours; wake to have deep thoughts – what were called the 'watches' of the night; and rest a while more before dawn.

Meanwhile you'll be experiencing physical changes. Sudden surges of energy run through your body. You may feel tingling in your arms and legs. Some people develop strange rashes; others find they can intentionally heal old conditions. Your skin and hair become more radiant. People comment that you're growing younger.

Your tastes in food may change: many people go off coffee and alcohol. As you become more spiritually aware, you're more sensitive to everything around you. You may find that you don't want to eat meat. This isn't a moral decision – your body is just reluctant to ingest certain foods. You'll probably experience changes in weight – slight gains or extreme losses. You'll need new clothes, which adds to your new self image.

You'll experience roller-coaster feelings. One time you're high, exultant, infused with light. You radiate such joy that strangers smile at you in the street. Another you're down, limbs shaking, cold with dread. A beast is gnawing at your stomach. There really seems no point in going on. Friends fret and recommend antidepressants. It's up to you if the roller-coaster highs are worth the lows.

Your senses are supra-naturally heightened. You're intensely aware of the beauty of creation. You notice every leaf on every tree. They seem symbolic of the abundance of creation. You start to wear clothes in brighter colours. Music becomes increasingly important to you. You may take up singing or playing a musical instrument. These changes happen as your senses adjust to perceive wider frequencies.

You experience heightened interpersonal awareness. You'll sense intuitively what the people around you are feeling. This doesn't come in words but as a radiation. The boundaries between you and others feel more permeable. You increasingly communicate with touches and hugs.

Paralleling these sensory changes come alterations in brain activity. You spend more time in a state of theta wave production. Some people experience very vivid dreams. Others find that meditation comes more easily. This is good because meditation is one of the best tools for spiritual development.

You may find that you are withdrawing from the world. You don't want to go out as often as before. It seems pointless to spend time and money on things that aren't important. You spend more time on reading, meditating, introspection. Conversely, when you go out you're fully engaged with the world around you. You strike up deep conversations with complete strangers. In this new state of spiritual awareness, you're intensely interested in life.

Whatever stage you're at, the cosmos conspires to help you. Messages appear everywhere – in books, in films, on billboards. Teachers turn up to guide you – either by inspiring or providing examples of what you don't want. You notice things that have a spiritual significance for you. You experience coincidences and synchronicities that defy any logical explanation. Small miracles manifest in your everyday world.

Your energy field interacts with things around you. Your phone dials an old friend who you rarely speak with. You have to do some work you hate and your computer suddenly shuts down. Learn to laugh and just don't fight it. Use the force to set up a protective energy field around those you love.

You have a heightened sense of integrity. Authenticity becomes of paramount importance. You have to be sincere in everything you do. Honesty becomes a priority in all your relationships. You cannot stay in a situation where you're not being true to yourself. You may have to leave your job or even your marriage. The decision seems inevitable since it is not a choice but a matter of principle.

Pulling all these things together is a deep sense of yearning. You experience what k.d. lang called 'constant craving'; the longing of the lover for their beloved; the burning of the soul separated from the divine. It's depicted in the Persian story of Majnun and Leyla. It's described in the writings of mystics like Rumi, St Teresa of Avila and Dante Alighieri.

This process is exhilarating, though not easy. In the end, the trauma will be worth it. Your passage through the darkness will leave you stronger. You'll garner the riches of your unconscious mind. That's why the Romans knew the god of the Underworld as Pluto, or Wealth. Stay true to your self and keep going. When the Japanese mend a broken pot, they fill the cracks with gold. They believe that when something has a history, it becomes more beautiful.

When you follow your soul's calling, you are finally expressing your true self. Despite the turmoil of awakening – or because of it – you become emotionally, psychologically and physically stronger. You feel in alignment with your soul's gift and your deep purpose. Be aware of what's happening and be careful. Guard those you love against any unintended consequences as you follow your soul story.

Brave New World

When you start to tell your soul story, you're stepping into a new reality. From now on, you'll do things differently. You'll meet new people, talk about different things. You'll go to other places, maybe even move home. In many ways it's entering a foreign land.

As you're creating a brave new world, there are some key things to explain. There are the people who inhabit this land. There are the historical events which shaped them. And there is the physical territory where the action takes place.

To appreciate this, look at *The Lord of the Rings*. Tolkien understood that to tell a good story, he had to give it firm foundations. He spent years devising charts, languages and backstories about Middle Earth. It's this that gives his stories such coherence. After this, he could introduce his main characters and get on with the action.

The same things apply to your soul story. The work you've done here provides foundations for your future. You've related the narrative of your life so far. You recognize the people who played a significant role. You've literally charted the terrain of your future. And you've done the other steps. You've worked out who you are, from your core values; and you've learned how to turn dreams through theory into action plans.

Here's a simple mnemonic for soul story work. It uses a five-point plan which you recall by relating it to your fingers. This gives you an easy way to remember these key factors. Life gets busy and it's easy to take your eyes off the target. If you're going to achieve your goals, it's vital to remember where you're going. Whenever you feel distracted or have a difficult decision to make, pause and focus on your priorities. Use this technique to remind yourself of your soul story.

Activity: Five Finger Technique

Let's look at how this works in a bit more detail. The trick is to associate each finger with one element of your story. Then you can run through them quickly to refresh the vision in your mind.

Start by giving a thumbs-up sign. Think about what this symbolizes: all's well, I'm alright. Link the thumb in your mind with your self. Remember the meditation when you met your future being. Recall how it felt to meet that person. When you hold up your thumb, you're identifying with your true self.

Your index finger indicates the way. Link it in your mind to where you're going. This can be a mental destination or a real place. Look at the map you drew showing your trajectory. Point your index finger to remind you where you're going.

The middle finger is the tallest digit. Use it as your prompt for action. See how it's divided into three sections: these represent the steps of fantasy -> theory -> plan. Remember your vision of the future, the excitement and anticipation you felt. For your dream to become reality, keep taking small steps towards that goal.

Your ring finger represents relationships. Let it remind you of the significant people in your life. When you touch this finger, focus on their being. Sense the energy that connects you over time and space. Feel awareness that they are always part of your story.

When two children say the same thing together, they link little fingers for luck. Let your little finger symbolize giving and receiving. Focus on your unique gift to the world. Touch your thumb and little finger to recall how this links with your core values.

In summary, then:

1. Thumb: symbolizes myself
2. Index finger: points to the map

3. Middle finger: dream, theory, plan
4. Ring finger: important relationships
5. Little finger: giving your gift

Use this mnemonic to remind yourself of key elements in your soul story.

Now and Forever

Soulwork involves connecting the physical, mental and spiritual worlds. Philosophical tradition in the West opposes mind and matter. Eastern mysticism unites them, but mystical insights transcend language so are hard to communicate. How else can you conceive the links between the phenomenal, the known and the cosmic realms?

Three bridges let us connect the seen and the unseen, the material and the transcendent worlds. These are mathematics, music and myth. The equations of mathematics, the harmonies of a musical score, the personifications in a myth: these let us glimpse the turning of the universe. We've mentioned the findings of quantum mathematics. Let's examine the other two modalities.

Myths are tales that have passed the test of time, surviving through repeated tellings and re-tellings. They reflect universal themes and fundamental truths, taking place in an everyworld and evertime. Myths are based on a narrative thread – events happen in a certain order. At the same time, they highlight patterns and relationships. They play with motif and repetition. They follow the same template as your soul story.

A myth is similar to a piece of music. They each use simple elements – a few basic themes, a limited range of notes – woven together to create new compositions. They can both be listened to repeatedly, giving something new each time. They depend on harmony and counterpoint, synchrony and balance. A myth plays with recurring themes: incidents reflect or contrast with each other. The hero and the villain often have much in common. In music, one instrument introduces a phrase and others echo it. A single note is deepened with a chord. The tune repeats but in a different key.

Music and myth follow rules, but they teach you to break

them. They are linear compositions which transcend sequential constraints. They raise you up so you can see great patterns unfolding. That is why music is so exhilarating. It takes you to a higher plane of existence. Music is pure energy made audible. It's cosmic power manifesting in your ears. It's the same force that grows a plant and drives the planets: it's truly called the music of the spheres.

When you think of it this way, everything is very simple. It all comes back to that unified energy field. The universe is a symphony of energies. All life is a dance to that cosmic sound. Your soul's call is to play your part in this creation. That's why the theme of your soulwork can be called your soul song.

Music transcends linear sequential time. It interweaves melody and harmony, letting you sense the patterns that underlie the form. Each chord in a tune is the intersection of time and eternity. You don't listen to a song for the last note. The parts all contribute to the whole. You enjoy each verse and chorus. You dance while the music lasts. It's the same with your soul story.

When you started working on your soul story, you began by visioning the future. This image helped you clarify your direction. It gave you a goal and some insight into how you'd get there. But that was just a checkpoint: a milestone on the greater journey. Maybe you sometimes ask yourself: Will it all be worthwhile? What will happen in the end?

The ending is often the first part of a story to be written. That sounds paradoxical, but actually it's perfectly reasonable. Think how a novel or play is structured. *Pride and Prejudice* is a romantic comedy: it's about Elizabeth and Darcy getting together. *Hamlet* is a tragedy: it's never going to turn out well. The author knows from the start who the main characters are and how the plot will turn out. All they have work out is the details of the journey.

The same is true of your soul story. This makes sense if you think about how it's structured. A soul story works on many different levels. It weaves together people, places and experiences. It creates bonds that traverse time and space. It values synchronicity over causal sequence. It's less about explanation and more about the perception of meaning.

It makes sense if the end is implicit in the story. That's not to say that it can't be changed. You are the author: you decide what's going to happen. What it does mean is that the outcome is a part of the process. If they are both co-determined, this moment is just as important as the last.

Why does this matter? Because it makes now all-important. If the end affects the beginning, then the process is a reflection of the end. It's no good waiting for some promised future. All you can do is live here in the present moment. Appreciate it and make the most of living. Now is all we have and all we need to know.

All the great mystics have told us something similar. The point of life is living. The voyager's purpose is to travel. Consider this in relation to your soul story. It's not just that you should wake up and smell the roses. Your destination is a mirror of the journey. Spend your days so that the pattern is congruent.

This insight is put nicely by Michael Singer. If you had an appointment with Death tonight, how would you live differently today? How about if it was in one week? What would you do to make the most of that time? Suppose Death turns up a year from now and you say, 'Where's my one week warning?' And Death says, 'You've had fifty-two weeks this year. And all the years before that. Didn't you know that you were going to die?'

So live your life with passion and integrity. Know that you have a unique path to follow. Find your gift and express it wholeheartedly. Let your days be filled with energy and purpose. Yet at the same time, exist in the moment. Love while you can. Give when you can. Dance in the rain. Sing your soul song.

Making A Start

When I sat down to write this book, I was unsure where to begin. So I decided to start at the end, right here.

There's an old joke about how it's hard to begin a journey.

A traveller has lost his way in the countryside.
He sees an old man leaning on a gate, and hails him:
"Can you tell me how to reach Kilcarnie from here?"
The old man pauses, chewing ruminatively on a straw.
"If I was going there, I wouldn't start from here..."

We all know that feeling. It's always hard to start a project. There are always other things that seem more pressing. Today I should really have done some exercise, I haven't been running for awhile. I'm meeting Susan at eleven: she's visiting from Singapore, so I don't want to be late. I've decided to write a new book, but I'm not sure where to begin. Besides, I'm learning to play guitar and my fingers are numb, so it will be hard to type. If I do some creative visualization later, perhaps I'll get some really good ideas. Maybe I'm not MEANT to start writing today. Suppose the universe is telling me something. Should I should wait for inspiration to strike...?

This all sounds very reasonable. But it's a 'red herring', a distraction from the real business in hand. When you're planning something that really matters, of course it can seem overwhelming. Not doing anything is a sort of safety mechanism, isn't it: by not taking the risk, you make sure that you'll never actually fail. There's a scene in the film *Bad Timing* set at a ritzy party. The men are all in sharp suits, the women in glamorous dresses. Leaning against the wall, one man watches a beautiful girl come down the staircase. As she passes, he says to her: "If we leave it at this, it always could have been perfect..."

If you leave your life at this, it always could have been perfect. The measure of a man is not what he is, but what he could have been. How poignant, how romantic... no, actually how sad. Because if you don't try, you'll never achieve anything. Personally I prefer the approach of the inventor Thomas Edison. When he finally got his theory to work, he was asked how he'd kept going after so many failed experiments. Edison replied, "I didn't fail: I just discovered a thousand ways not to make an electric light bulb."

Now that's a good attitude to have.

It's never easy to start work on your soul story. How much simpler to postpone until the conditions are perfect. When do you think that will be? Next month, in a year, if you move house... that sounds rather like the Red Queen talking to Alice in Wonderland: Jam yesterday, jam tomorrow, but never jam today.

The truth is that conditions will never be absolutely right. There will always be something to stop you, something more urgent, something you need to learn first. Don't get waylaid by such blandishments. Schedule time so you can fulfil other commitments. Learn new skills as you go along. Don't confront, don't argue, don't justify: just quietly begin doing what you're meant to be doing. Start singing the song you were born to sing.

Yes, at times it will feel daunting. It will feel like you've taken on far more than you can handle. You'll sit amidst the packing cases, physically or metaphorically, and wonder how you ever reached this point. You'll wonder if it's worth going on. You may even ask yourself whether you should go back. At least your old life was comfortably familiar: better the devil you know...

But I'm telling you that's no way to think. The truth is that you couldn't go back even if you wanted to. You see, you're not the person you used to be. You've moved on, grown and changed. If you step back, it will feel quite different from how you imagine. The past is another country, they do things differently there.

And you're not alone. Sometimes it will feel like you're lost in a dark forest. You can't go back, you can't see forwards and you feel very scared. In those hardest times, lift up your head and look around you. The night may be very black and you might not know which way to go. But when you look up, you'll see little lights in the darkness. Those are others who are working on their own stories. They can't show you where to go, but they can keep you company in the dark woods.

Each of us must make our own way and carry our own lantern. Your soul story is personal to you: if you try to follow someone else's way, you'll end up where they are – and please believe me that it won't feel AT ALL like it looks from where you're standing now. You're creating something that suits you much better and which will make you much happier.

Life has dealt you four aces; decide if you want to play them low or high. You can't get to happily ever after if you don't start with before. The point of life is to die with memories, not dreams.

The longest journey starts with the first few steps.

A never-ending story begins with the first words.

End Note

You've come a long way since your soul began to wake. You know that you're on the right track because of the excitement in your heart. Now you're living your life with passion and purpose. You're singing your soul song.

Nothing is wasted and nothing is lost. All the experiences you've had brought you to where you are today. The things that happened made you who you are. The people who matter are always in your life. The places you've been form the backdrop to your never-ending story.

Now the story all makes sense. What was lost is found. What was broken becomes whole. The stars in the sky make a pattern. You see eternity in an hour and infinity in a grain of sand. You're living your soul story.

Go well.

As You Travel

May the way be smooth before you
The skies shine clear above you
The wind be always at your back

May you have fire bright to warm you
Good friendships to cheer you
Food to break your fast

May you have work for your hands
Books to nourish your mind
Music to lift your soul

Jane Bailey Bain 9/12/2015
In the Celtic blessing tradition

Acknowledgements

Thanks to the friends who make me feel more like myself, especially:

Susan Welsh
Jeri and Rita
Emmanuelle
Jo Hackett
Steve Morse

About the Author

Jane Bailey Bain is an author, speaker and creative coach. She was born in the United States and grew up in Geneva. She studied Psychology (MA) at Oxford University and Anthropology (MSc) at the London School of Economics. After travelling extensively around the world, Jane trained as a business consultant with IBM. She worked for several years as an advisor on development projects in Asia and Africa, specializing in social issues. During this time she became interested in stories and how people use them in everyday life. On her return to London, Jane set up a series of courses on Mythology, Story Structure and Creative Writing. These combine psychological and anthropological approaches to myth and storytelling. Jane holds a PGCE in Adult Education and a Certificate in Counselling Skills. She is the author of *LifeWorks: Using myth and archetype to develop your life story* and *StoryWorks: A Handbook for Leaders, Writers and Speakers*.

SoulWorks draws on profound insights from psychology, anthropology and spirituality. Jane's approach is rooted in story analysis and life trajectory. She combines this with a wide range of practical tools and techniques. These help you actualize your dreams into future plans and goals.

Start the journey at www.janebaileybain.com

BOOKS

O-BOOKS

SPIRITUALITY

O is a symbol of the world, of oneness and unity; this eye represents knowledge and insight. We publish titles on general spirituality and living a spiritual life. We aim to inform and help you on
your own journey in this life. ,
If you have enjoyed this book, why not tell other readers by post-
ing a review on your preferred book site?

Recent bestsellers from O-Books are:

Heart of Tantric Sex
Diana Richardson
Revealing Eastern secrets of deep love and intimacy to Western couples.
Paperback: 978-1-90381-637-0 ebook: 978-1-84694-637-0

Crystal Prescriptions
The A-Z guide to over 1,200 symptoms and their healing crystals
Judy Hall
The first in the popular series of six books, this handy little guide is packed as tight as a pill-bottle with crystal remedies for ailments.
Paperback: 978-1-90504-740-6 ebook: 978-1-84694-629-5

Take Me To Truth
Undoing the Ego
Nouk Sanchez, Tomas Vieira
The best-selling step-by-step book on shedding the Ego, using the teachings of A Course In Miracles.
Paperback: 978-1-84694-050-7 ebook: 978-1-84694-654-7

The 7 Myths about Love...Actually!
The journey from your HEAD to the HEART of your SOUL
Mike George
Smashes all the myths about LOVE.
Paperback: 978-1-84694-288-4 ebook: 978-1-84694-682-0

The Holy Spirit's Interpretation of the New Testament
A course in Understanding and Acceptance
Regina Dawn Akers
Following on from the strength of A Course In Miracles, NTI teaches us how to experience the love and oneness of God.
Paperback: 978-1-84694-085-9 ebook: 978-1-78099-083-5

The Message of A Course In Miracles
A translation of the text in plain language
Elizabeth A. Cronkhite
ition of *A Course in Miracles* into plain, everyday language
he seeking inner peace. The companion volume, *Practicing A
ourse In Miracles*, offers practical lessons and mentoring.
Paperback: 978-1-84694-319-5 ebook: 978-1-84694-642-4

Rising in Love
My Wild and Crazy Ride to Here and Now, with Amma, the
Hugging Saint
Ram Das Batchelder
Rising in Love conveys an author's extraordinary journey of
spiritual awakening with the Guru, Amma.
Paperback: 978-1-78279-687-9 ebook: 978-1-78279-686-2

Thinker's Guide to God
Peter Vardy
An introduction to key issues in the philosophy of religion.
Paperback: 978-1-90381-622-6

Your Simple Path
Find happiness in every step
Ian Tucker
A guide to helping us reconnect with what is really important in
our lives.
Paperback: 978-1-78279-349-6 ebook: 978-1-78279-348-9

365 Days of Wisdom
Daily Messages To Inspire You Through The Year
Dadi Janki
Daily messages which cool the mind, warm the heart and guide
you along your journey.
Paperback: 978-1-84694-863-3 ebook: 978-1-84694-864-0

Body of Wisdom
Women's Spiritual Power and How it Serves
Hilary Hart
Bringing together the dreams and experiences of women across the world with today's most visionary spiritual teachers.
Paperback: 978-1-78099-696-7 ebook: 978-1-78099-695-0

Dying to Be Free
From Enforced Secrecy to Near Death to True Transformation
Hannah Robinson
After an unexpected accident and near-death experience, Hannah Robinson found herself radically transforming her life, while a remarkable new insight altered her relationship with her father; a practising Catholic priest.
Paperback: 978-1-78535-254-6 ebook: 978-1-78535-255-3

The Ecology of the Soul
A Manual of Peace, Power and Personal Growth for Real People in the Real World
Aidan Walker
Balance your own inner Ecology of the Soul to regain your natural state of peace, power and wellbeing.
Paperback: 978-1-78279-850-7 ebook: 978-1-78279-849-1

Not I, Not other than I
The Life and Teachings of Russel Williams
Steve Taylor, Russel Williams
The miraculous life and inspiring teachings of one of the World's greatest living Sages.
Paperback: 978-1-78279-729-6 ebook: 978-1-78279-728-9

On the Other Side of Love
A Woman's Unconventional Journey Towards Wisdom
Muriel Maufroy
When life has lost all meaning, what do you do?
Paperback: 978-1-78535-281-2 ebook: 978-1-78535-282-9

Practicing A Course In Miracles
A Translation of the Workbook in Plain Language and With
Mentoring Notes
Elizabeth A. Cronkhite
The practical second and third volumes of The Plain-Language
A Course In Miracles.
Paperback: 978-1-84694-403-1 ebook: 978-1-78099-072-9

Quantum Bliss
The Quantum Mechanics of Happiness, Abundance, and Health
George S. Mentz
Quantum Bliss is the breakthrough summary of success and
spirituality secrets that customers have been waiting for.
Paperback: 978-1-78535-203-4 ebook: 978-1-78535-204-1

The Upside Down Mountain
Mags MacKean
A must-read for anyone weary of chasing success and happiness
– one woman's inspirational journey swapping the uphill slog for
the downhill slope.
Paperback: 978-1-78535-171-6 ebook: 978-1-78535-172-3

Your Personal Tuning Fork
The Endocrine System
Deborah Bates
Discover your body's health secret, the endocrine system, and
'twang' your way to sustainable health!
Paperback: 978-1-84694-503-8 ebook: 978-1-78099-697-4

Readers of ebooks can buy or view any of these bestsellers by clicking on the live link in the title. Most titles are published in paperback and as an ebook. Paperbacks are available in traditional bookshops. Both print and ebook formats are available online.

Find more titles and sign up to our readers' newsletter at http://www.johnhuntpublishing.com/mind-body-spirit

Follow us on Facebook at https://www.facebook.com/OBooks/ and Twitter at https://twitter.com/obooks